30-minute
kids'cakes

30-minute kids' cakes

Sara Lewis

Bounty
Books

Dedication

To my fabulous mother, for her memorable cakes and childhood parties that were always such good fun – what a role model!

First published in Great Britain in 2002 by
Hamlyn, a division of Octopus Publishing Group Ltd

This edition published in 2006 by Bounty Books,
a division of Octopus Publishing Group Ltd
2–4 Heron Quays, London E14 4JP
An Hachette Livre UK Company
Reprinted 2006, 2007 (twice)
Copyright © Octopus Publishing Group Ltd 2002

ISBN: 978-0-753713-71-6

A CIP catalogue record for this book is available from the British Library.

Printed and bound in China

Notes

Standard level spoon measures are used in all recipes
1 tablespoon = one 15 ml spoon
1 teaspoon = one 5 ml spoon

Both metric and imperial measurements are given for the recipes. Use one set of measures only, not a mixture of both.

Ovens should be preheated to the specified temperature. If using a fan assisted oven, follow the manufacturer's instructions for adjusting the time and temperature.

Medium eggs have been used throughout.

contents

It wouldn't be a birthday party without a cake, but if you're a working mum with young children, as I am, it can sometimes seem like the last thing you can fit into a busy schedule.

Cakes needn't take very long to decorate, especially if you make and freeze a sponge base in advance or cheat and buy ready-made cakes. A child has no idea if you've been fiddling around in the kitchen, up to your eyes in icing sugar for evening after evening or for just 30 minutes – it's that first eye-catching glance that counts. Kids love bright colours, sweets and candles. Just as you can buy the cake itself, some decorations can be bought too, and it was as a result of my making the Construction Site Cake (see page 70) for my son William's sixth birthday, covered with a pack of new yellow diggers and trucks, that the idea for this book was born.

I have always admired those complicated royal-iced cakes covered with intricate piped detail, but they require specialist equipment, not to mention time and expertise. Busy people need things that are easy to buy and use. All the cake ingredients in this book can be picked up on the supermarket run. You will probably have most of the cake tins and any other equipment needed in your kitchen cupboard, but any extras are readily available from your local hardware or department store. Cake boards, colourings, cutters and ready-to-roll icing are very often cheaper and can be available in a greater selection from a specialist cake-decorating supplier. Look for your local shop in the telephone directory – they are often located at a distance from local shopping centres or malls, but are well worth a detour and some even provide a mail-order service.

The novelty cakes on the pages to come are all quick and easy to make. If you can roll out pastry, then you can roll out ready-to-roll icing. If you haven't used this before, it will prove a great discovery. It can be coloured in a multitude of tones, and any imperfections that arise can be smoothed away with your fingertips dusted in cornflour or icing sugar. Plus, there are lots of butter-iced cakes.

We've something for everyone, from tiny cakes for tiny toddlers, to something pretty and flowery, a selection of mean machines and something scary for Halloween. But you don't have to wait for a birthday to make one of these cakes – the decorated fairy cakes are great to take into school fund-raising days, or just to make for fun on a wet afternoon after school. Whatever the occasion, I do hope you and your children will get as much pleasure from these cakes as my children and I have had in trying out the many ideas.

the basics

getting started

equipment

Since all the cakes in this book are quick and easy to assemble, the amount of equipment needed is quite minimal. The items required will probably be ones that you have already in the kitchen, such as a rolling pin, a serrated knife for cutting cakes, a round-bladed knife or small palette knife for spreading jam or butter icing, a small, sharp knife for trimming icing, plus a pastry brush or a large, new artist's brush for brushing away excess icing sugar or cornflour. A child's small rolling pin is perfect for rolling out tiny amounts of coloured icing details. If you don't have one, it is well worth buying one, along with a small sieve for dusting icing sugar on to the work surface and a new, fine paintbrush, useful for 'gluing' icing details on to cakes with jam or water. A selection of different sized biscuit cutters is invaluable.

▼ *A selection of the basic equipment required for cake making and decorating.*

basic equipment

- kitchen scales
- rolling pin
- serrated knife
- round-bladed knife or palette knife
- small sharp knife
- pastry brush
- artist's paintbrushes
- scissors
- small and large sieves
- bowls
- baking tins (see page 14)
- nonstick baking paper
- small rolling pin (child's or craft)

▼ *An everyday round-bladed knife is ideal for spreading butter icing on to little cakes.*

▲ Individual cakes can be cut from a basic traybake sponge cake, cooked in a roasting tin (see page 20), using a huge range of animal, number or alphabet cutters.

▲ Look for plain-coloured paper cases or patterned foil cases from good cookshops or specialist cake-decorating shops .

ingredients

To make life easier,the following ingredients are used regularly to decorate the cakes in this book, so it may be a good idea to keep them in stock:

- butter
- margarine
- plain flour
- self-raising flour
- baking powder
- caster sugar
- vanilla essence
- lemons
- cocoa powder

- icing sugar
- ready-to-roll icing
- apricot jam
- cornflour
- chocolate
- paste and liquid food colours
- tubes of writing icing
- selection of cake decorations
- sweets

▲ Tubes of ready-made writing icing come in four primary colours and save all that fiddly making of greaseproof-paper piping bags.

special equipment

Some of the cakes require special equipment. These items can often be purchased in supermarkets, cookshops or cake-decorating shops. Versatile fancy cutters, for example, can be used time and time again.

- piping bags
- various metal or plastic cutters – alphabet, numbers, shapes
- different shaped plunger cuttes (see below)
- cake boards

piping bags

To make a piping bag, cut a square piece of greaseproof paper. Fold it in half diagonally to make a triangle, then make a small mark halfway along the longest side of the triangle. Place your fingernail at this mark, then curl the point of the triangle on the same edge around to the next point so that your fingernail mark becomes the base of the piping bag or cone. Repeat with the other point and fold the top edge down several times to secure the piping bag. Fill the bag, fold down to stop the filling oozing out during use and snip off the tip with scissors ready for piping.

cutters

Cutters are a simple yet very effective way of adding interest and impact to the most basic cakes, be they individual fairy cakes or large multi-tiered sponge cakes. Look for ones in a range of sizes and shapes. They will keep for years if looked after properly – make sure you wash and dry them well after use.

When using small cutters:
- dip them in cornflour or a little icing sugar before use so that icing shapes don't stick.
- to release icing shapes, press them out of the cutter with a fingertip or rounded end of a small brush.
- wash cutters after use with a small bottle brush and dry in the bottom of a cooling oven so that the joins do not rust.
- store cutters in the tin that they came in, or a small plastic box – as they are small, they are easy to lose.

▲ *Tiny plunger cutters, often described as aspic cutters, are available in flower blossom and heart shapes and can be obtained from good cookshops or specialist cake-decorating shops. Use them to stamp out miniature shapes, quickly and easily, from rolled-out icing. Press shapes into a round of foam or a new washing-up sponge so that the flowers curl and look more realistic. See also the Flower Garden cakes on page 72.*

cake boards

Cake boards come in a wide range of sizes, shapes and thicknesses. Thin boards have been used in the book, but thicker drums may also be used if you like.

Cake boards needn't be thrown away after use. Simply scrape off any leftover cake and icing and clean the board with a damp dish-cloth. When dry, cover any scratches with a sheet of foil or use white, plain or marbled coloured ready-to-roll icing. If using icing, leave it to harden before positioning the cake. Alternatively, spread a little melted chocolate or butter icing over the board instead.

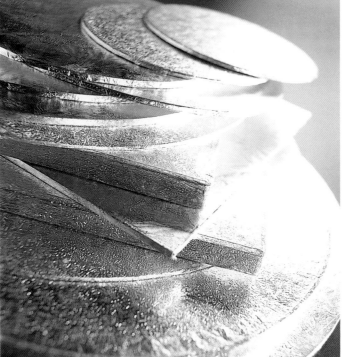

❧ Containers of metal number or alphabet cutters are useful if you have young children. Look out for mixed packs of stars, hearts, animals, mixed shapes and the basic rounds and squares in various sizes.

▲ Plastic biscuit cutters are available in all kinds of shapes. They are less expensive than metal ones but not as durable. You may find these cutters in children's modelling sets along with a small child's rolling pin, which is invaluable when rolling out tiny portions of icing for facial features.

◀ Cake boards are most often sold covered with a silver covering, but may also be available in gold, green or red or even with Christmas motifs on them. Look out for them in supermarkets, good stationers, cookshops and specialist cake-decorating shops.

bakeware

If you are making a decorated party cake, there is nothing as delicious as a home-made cake. Before you start, check the cake recipe to see which size and shape of tin you require. Lining a tin is an important first step to a perfectly turned-out cake.

choosing a cake tin

The baking tins used in the book are all widely available in good cookshops, hardware stores or in the kitchenware section of large department stores. Choose from:

12-section mini- and standard-sized muffin tin
12-section bun tray
15 cm (6 inch) Victoria Sandwich tin
18 cm (7 inch) Victoria Sandwich tin
20 cm (8 inch) deep, square tin
23 cm (9 inch) deep, round tin, with or without a loose base
30 x 23 x 5 cm (12 x 9 x 2 inch) roasting tin
18 x 7 x 5 cm (7 x 3 x 2 inch) or 500 g (1 lb) loaf tin

Avoid budget-priced cake tins from money-saving stores or mail-order catalogues, as these can be very thin and will dent easily. A good tin should last you 20 years or more, so why not buy the best?

If you are starting from scratch or plan to make a lot of cakes, then look for a multi-sized square cake tin (see top right), which is also available in a round version. Simply adjust the straight sides and dividers on the square tin for a variety of cake sizes and, when not in use, unclip the sides and store the tin flat – ideal if kitchen storage space is tight.

The round cake tin has an adjustable ring, so it can be used to make cakes from 15–23 cm (6–9 inches). Both tins are available from good cookshops or department stores.

QUICK TIP

★ Always measure a cake tin across the base, as many have a lip around the top or sloping sides which can disguise the tin's true size.

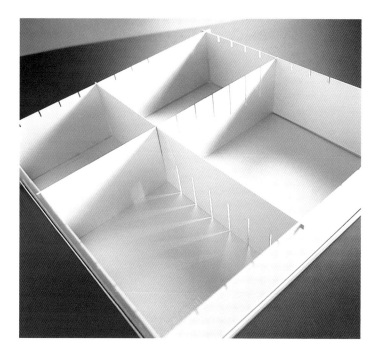

▲ *One multi-sized, square cake tin can be adjusted to make a variety of cake sizes.*

▼ *For perfect results, purchase a selection of good quality cake tins.*

preparing cake tins

Fairy cake or bun trays and muffin tins are the easiest to prepare. Simply pop a paper case into each section and you're ready to go. However, the preparation for larger cakes takes just a few minutes longer. Tins for large, shallow cakes, such as a traditional Victoria sandwich, require a light brushing with sunflower or vegetable oil and a circle of greaseproof paper in the base, again brushed with oil. Larger, deeper cakes require a tin with a base lining, plus paper around the edges.

If you use nonstick baking paper, there's no need to grease the tin first or brush the paper once the tin has been lined.

Whether you are lining a round or square tin, the method is the same: use a double thickness of paper for the sides, a little wider than the height of the tin and a little longer than the circumference. Fold one side of the paper over to make a 1 cm (½ inch) lip and snip at intervals. If using a square tin, stand the paper in the tin so that the snipped edge is on the base and crease the paper into the corners. Using the tin as a guide, draw around it on the baking paper, cut out the circle or square and press it into the base of the tin so that it fits snugly.

For a roasting tin, use a very large sheet of nonstick baking paper and snip the corners. Press the paper into the tin so that the cut edges of the paper sit in the corners neatly.

▲ *Line the sides and the base of a deep round or square tin with separate pieces of nonstick baking paper or greased, greaseproof paper. Make small cuts along one side of the paper for the sides, so that it fits snugly around curved edges or into corners.*

▲ *For shallower cake tins, such as a roasting tin, simply snip into the corners of a large piece of nonstick baking paper or greased greaseproof paper and press it into the base of the tin so that the paper fits snugly into the sides and the corners of the tin.*

making your own cakes

first steps

Anyone can make a cake. There's nothing easier than an all-in-one cake, where all the ingredients are put into a bowl and beaten for just a couple of minutes until smooth. Make sure you keep to either metric or imperial measurements, rather than using a mixture of the two. Self-raising flour with a little added baking powder will give an extra boost, resulting in a nicely risen cake, providing, of course, it's in the right sized tin. Too large a tin, and no amount of careful mixing will make a generously deep cake. For cakes that use more than four eggs, it is easier to handle quantities if the fat and sugar are creamed together first, rather than using an all-in-one method.

When baking, try to resist the temptation to keep opening the oven door to check the progress, as the rush of cold air may make the cake sink in the middle. Set the timer for 5 minutes less than the specified time and then check. Ovens vary in temperature, even on the same setting, and fan-assisted ovens are particularly fast. Manufacturers recommend reducing the temperature by 10 degrees or by 10 minutes' cooking time if using a fan oven, so check the handbook or use an oven thermometer, available from good cookshops or hardware stores.

is my cake cooked?

If your cake looks well risen and golden but you're not sure if it is ready, test large cakes by inserting a skewer into the centre. If the skewer comes out cleanly with no smears of cake mixture on it, the cake is ready. If not, return it to the oven and test again after another 5–10 minutes. If the cake looks the right colour, even though it's not done in the middle, cover it loosely with foil to prevent over-browning, especially if you have a fan-assisted oven, and return it to the oven.

Test little cakes by pressing the tops lightly with your fingertips. If the cakes spring back, they're ready.

getting ahead

If your child is having a large birthday tea with a crowd of friends, it can be a great help to make the birthday cake in advance. Pack the cooled, cooked cake, without icing, in a plastic box, seal, label and freeze for up to 6 weeks. Interleave sandwich cakes with greaseproof paper so that they can be separated easily. Alternatively, wrap in foil or clingfilm and place in a freezer-proof bag. Loosen the wrappings and thaw at room temperature for 3 hours.

Fairy cakes also freeze well and, if you have 2 bun trays, then it really doesn't take more than a few extra minutes to make a double batch. Turn the cakes out of the trays, cool, then pack into a large plastic box. Seal, label and freeze as above. Decorate while still frozen then leave at room temperature for about an hour to thaw completely.

ways to cheat

Most large supermarkets sell a wide range of ready-made cakes. These are a great standby if you're pushed for time or have a dread of baking. Look for thick slices of Madeira cake or layered angel cake, round sandwich cakes, chocolate marble loaf cakes, multi-size Swiss rolls, either jam-filled or fondant-filled, plain or chocolate sponges, fruit cakes and tiny fairy cakes – the choice seems endless. The recipes in this book suggest particular cakes, but by all means swap types, providing you keep to the same shape and size.

▶ *Choose from a selection of bought cakes as a basis for the novelty cakes in this book. At the top, a choc-chip sponge cake, below a striped angel cake, a plain slab of Madeira cake and below that a chocolate marble cake and a slice of fruit cake.*

basic cake recipes

In spite of its attractive appearance, a decorated cake still has to taste good. A number of delicious, yet simple, cake recipes are used for the decorated cakes in this book and, if you choose to make your own, make sure that you follow the cake instructions carefully. For perfect results, always weigh out ingredients accurately.

mini cup cakes

Makes 12

50 g (2 oz) soft margarine
50 g (2 oz) caster sugar
50 g (2 oz) self-raising flour
1 egg

1 Put all the cake ingredients into a bowl or food processor and beat, or process, until smooth.

2 Divide the mixture between a 12-hole, mini muffin tray lined with petit-four cases.

3 Bake in a preheated oven, 180°C (350°F), Gas Mark 4, for 10–13 minutes.

FLAVOUR VARIATIONS
vanilla: Add ½ teaspoon vanilla essence.
citrus: Add 1 teaspoon each grated orange and grated lemon rind or 2 teaspoons of a single fruit rind.
chocolate: Substitute 1 tablespoon cocoa powder for 1 tablespoon of the flour.

❚ *For a simple all-in-one cake put all the ingredients into a bowl and beat with a wooden spoon. Alternatively, process in an electric mixer or food processor until smooth.*

fairy cakes

Makes 12, or 2 x 15 cm (6 inch) Victoria sandwich cakes, if you add ½ teaspoon baking powder

125 g (4 oz) soft margarine
125 g (4 oz) caster sugar
125 g (4 oz) self-raising flour
2 eggs

1 Put all the cake ingredients into a bowl or food processor and beat, or process, until smooth.

2 Divide the mixture between a 12-hole bun tray lined with paper cake cases or, alternatively, 2 greased and base-lined round sandwich tins.

3 Bake in a preheated oven, 180°C (350°F), Gas Mark 4, for 15–18 minutes.

FLAVOUR VARIATIONS
vanilla: Add 1 teaspoon vanilla essence.
citrus: Add 2 teaspoons each grated lemon and grated orange rind or the grated rind of one medium orange.
chocolate: Substitute 2 tablespoons cocoa powder for 2 tablespoons of the flour.

victoria sandwich cake

Makes 2 x 18 cm (7 inch) cakes

175 g (6 oz) soft margarine
175 g (6 oz) caster sugar
175 g (6 oz) self-raising flour
½ teaspoon baking powder
3 eggs
3 tablespoons jam or half quantity Butter Icing
(see pages 22–23)

1 Put all the cake ingredients into a bowl or food processor and beat until smooth.

2 Spoon the mixture into 2 x 18 cm (7 inch) greased and base-lined sandwich tins. Level the tops with a palette knife.

3 Bake in a preheated oven, 180°C (350°F), Gas Mark 4, for 20–25 minutes.

4 Turn out the cakes and leave to cool, then fill with jam or butter icing.

FLAVOUR VARIATIONS
vanilla: Add 1 teaspoon vanilla essence.
citrus: Add 3 teaspoons each grated lemon and grated orange rind or the grated rind of one large fruit.
chocolate: Reduce the quantity of flour to 150 g (5 oz) and add 25 g (1 oz) cocoa powder.

◄ *The three most popular cake flavourings are grated lemon or orange rind, vanilla essence and cocoa powder for a chocolate taste.*

madeira cake

Makes 1 x 23 cm (9 inch) deep, round cake
or 1 x 20 cm (8 inch) deep, square cake
or 30 x 23 x 5 cm (12 x 9 x 2 inch) traybake cake cooked
    in a roasting tin

250 g (8 oz) soft margarine
250 g (8 oz) caster sugar
4 eggs
2 tablespoons milk
300 g (10 oz) self-raising flour
1 teaspoon baking powder

1 Using a wooden spoon or electric whisk, cream the margarine and sugar together until light and fluffy. Lightly beat the eggs with the milk in a separate bowl. Mix the flour and baking powder together and gradually beat into the creamed mixture alternating with the egg and milk mixture.

2 Spoon the mixture into a tin lined on the base and sides with greased greaseproof or nonstick baking paper and level the surface with a palette knife.

3 Bake in a preheated oven, 160°C (325°F), Gas Mark 3, for 45–55 minutes for a round or square cake or until a skewer comes out cleanly, or for 30–35 minutes for a traybake cake or until the cake springs back when lightly pressed with your fingertips.

> **FLAVOUR VARIATIONS**
> vanilla: Add 1½ teaspoons vanilla essence.
> citrus: Add the grated rind of half a lemon and 1 orange and substitute fruit juice for the milk.
> chocolate: Substitute 40 g (1½ oz) cocoa powder for the same weight of flour and increase the quantity of baking powder to 1½ teaspoons.

loaf cake

Makes 1 x 500 g (1 lb) cake
or 18 x 7 x 5 cm (7 x 3 x 2 inch) cake

125 g (4 oz) soft margarine
125 g (4 oz) caster sugar
2 eggs
2 teaspoons milk
125 g (4 oz) self-raising flour
50 g (2 oz) plain flour

1 Cream the margarine and sugar together until light and fluffy using a wooden spoon or electric mixer. Lightly beat the eggs with the milk in a separate bowl. Mix the flours together and gradually fold into the creamed mixture, alternating with the egg and milk mixture. Continue mixing until smooth.

2 Spoon the mixture into a tin lined with a large piece of nonstick baking paper snipped into the corners so that the base and sides are lined (see page 15). Level the top of the mixture with a palette knife.

3 Bake in a preheated oven, 160°C (325°F), Gas Mark 3, for 45 minutes or until a skewer inserted into the centre of the cake comes out cleanly.

> **FLAVOUR VARIATIONS**
> vanilla: Add 1 teaspoon vanilla essence.
> citrus: Add the grated rind of half a medium orange and half a lemon.
> chocolate: Substitute 2 tablespoons cocoa powder for the same quantity of plain flour.

american muffins

Makes 12

300 g (10 oz) plain flour
3 teaspoons baking powder
125 g (4 oz) light muscovado sugar
3 eggs
4 tablespoons sunflower oil
50 g (2 oz) butter, melted
2 teaspoons vanilla essence
150 g (5 oz) natural yogurt

1 Put the flour, baking powder and sugar into a bowl. Add the eggs, oil, melted butter, vanilla essence and yogurt and mix together lightly with a fork.

2 Divide the mixture between a 12-hole deep muffin tin lined with paper muffin cases.

3 Bake in a preheated oven, 200°C (400°F), Gas Mark 6, for 15–18 minutes until the muffins are golden and well risen and the tops are slightly cracked.

FLAVOUR VARIATIONS
chocolate chip: Add 100 g (3½ oz) dark, milk or white chocolate drops at the end of mixing.
double choc: Omit the vanilla, substitute 25 g (1 oz) cocoa powder for the same amount of flour, and add 100 g (3½ oz) dark chocolate drops at the end of mixing.
banana: Use 1 teaspoon vanilla essence and add 1 mashed ripe banana with the eggs and oil.

basic icings

butter icing

Butter icing is easy to make and use with lots of differnet flabouts. It can be spread smooth or textured. Check your cake recipe and follow the chart opposite for the quantity of butter icing required. Butter icing can be flavoured with vanilla, lemon or orange, or chocolate; the chart opposite shows the amounts needed.

using butter icing

If you can butter a slice of bread, then you can decorate a cake with butter icing. The secret is to spread the cake with a very thin layer of icing first to stick the crumbs in place. Once you have done that, add a second, thicker layer of icing and spread it smooth as in the Piggy Bank (see below), the Mermaid (see page 74) or leave it with a slightly ruffled effect, which is ideal if making 'water' (see page 80) or an animal cake, such as the Easter Chicks (see page 104).

► *It is important to sift the icing sugar thoroughly, so that the butter icing is perfectly smooth.*

▼ *My First Piggy Bank (see page 90) has been spread smoothly with two layers of butter icing.*

MAKING BUTTER ICING

To make butter icing, put the butter into a bowl (bring the butter to room temperature first for easy mixing) and gradually beat in the sifted icing sugar and milk with a wooden spoon, electric whisk or food processor until light and fluffy. Stir in the flavouring and colouring. The table below provides ingredients for making varying amounts of icing.

ingredients	*single quantity*	*double quantity*	*triple quantity*	*quadruple quantity*
butter	50 g (2 oz)	125 g (4 oz)	175 g (6 oz)	250 g (8 oz)
icing sugar	125 g (4 oz)	250 g (8 oz)	375 g (12 oz)	500 g (1 lb)
milk	1 teaspoon	2 teaspoons	3 teaspoons	4 teaspoons

FLAVOUR VARIATIONS

This table provides you with different quantities of the basic flavour variations used in these cakes: vanilla, citrus and chocolate.
For vanilla-flavoured icing, add the appropriate quantity of vanilla essence. **For citrus-flavoured icing**, substitute the appropriate quantity of grated orange or lemon rind and orange or lemon juice instead of the milk.
For chocolate-flavoured icing, omit the milk and substitute the appropriate quantity of cocoa powder mixed to a paste with an equal quantity of boiling water (i.e. mix 1 tablespoon cocoa powder with 1 tablespoon boiling water).

flavour	*single quantity*	*double quantity*	*triple quantity*	*quadruple quantity*
vanilla	½ teaspoon essence	1 teaspoon essence	1½ teaspoons essence	2 teaspoons essence
citrus	2 teaspoons rind, plus juice instead of milk	4 teaspoons rind, plus juice instead of milk	6 teaspoons rind, plus juice instead of milk	8 teaspoons rind, plus juice instead of milk
chocolate	1 tablespoon cocoa powder dissolved in 1 tablespoon of water	2 tablespoons cocoa powder dissolved in 2 tablespoons of waters	3 tablespoons cocoa powder dissolved in 3 tablespoons of waters	4 tablespoons cocoa powder dissolved in 4 tablespoons of waters

ready-to-roll icing

It is very simple to make your own ready-to-roll icing. You may need to order the liquid glucose from a chemist's shop. Don't be tempted to leave it out, as it is crucial for the icing's elasticity. Available in a variety of pot sizes, it will keep for several months in a cool place, if well sealed.

Basic quantity
1 large egg white
2 tablespoons liquid glucose
500 g (1lb) icing sugar, sifted

Mix the egg white and glucose in a large bowl. Gradually beat in the icing sugar using a wooden spoon, kneading it in with your hands when it becomes too stiff to stir. Colour as required then wrap the icing tightly in a plastic bag until ready to use.

Note: Eggs should never be eaten raw by children, pregnant women, the elderly or those recovering from serious illness unless pasteurized. Look out for pasteurized eggs in the supermarket chiller cabinet, but if these are unavailable then make up powdered egg white (sold in tubs in the baking ingredients section) as the pack directs and use this instead.

QUICK TIPS

★ Liquid glucose is a clear syrup, similar to golden syrup. If it is very stiff, first warm it in the microwave in a suitable container for 20–30 seconds on full power then measure the basic quantity above as needed, and use an electric food mixer when making larger quantities.

★ Wrap the icing as soon as possible after making, or it will dry out and crack when moulding.

★ If you'd rather not make your own icing, but can't find ready-to-roll icing in the shops, you can use white marzipan instead.

white chocolate fudge frosting

Covers one 23 cm (9 inch) deep cake (see page 34)
Used for Dot-to-dot (see page 34)

200 g (7 oz) luxury white cooking chocolate
175 g (6 oz) icing sugar, sifted
2 tablespoons milk

Break the chocolate into pieces and melt in a heatproof bowl set over a saucepan of just simmering water. Add the icing sugar and 1 tablespoon of the milk and mix to a smooth, thick paste. Stir in the remaining milk and beat well. Quickly spread the frosting over the cake while it is still warm, and add the decorations if using.

dark chocolate fudge frosting

Covers 6 fairy cakes (see Chocolate Hedgehogs, page 100)

25 g (1 oz) butter
15 g (½ oz) cocoa powder
175 g (6 oz) icing sugar
2 tablespoons milk
pinch of ground cinnamon

Melt the butter in a small saucepan. Stir in the cocoa powder and cook, stirring constantly, for 30 seconds until smooth. Remove the pan from the heat and gradually stir in the icing sugar (no need to sift) and milk, mixing until smooth. Add the cinnamon and return the frosting to the heat for 1 minute, stirring constantly until it has a glossy pouring consistency. Quickly spread the frosting over the cakes while it is still warm.

QUICK TIP

★ Unlike ready-to-roll and butter icings, chocolate frosting must be spread over the cake while it is still warm. As it cools, it thickens. If the icing cools to leave knife marks, simply dip a round-bladed or palette knife into boiling water, dry it and then spread the icing. The heat of the knife works like magic to smooth out any lines.

chocolate ganache

Covers 8 rabbits (see page 108)
Or to cover a 23 cm (9 inch) deep round cake

300 ml (½ pint) double cream
25 g (1 oz) butter
300 g (10 oz) luxury dark chocolate, broken into pieces

Put the cream into a saucepan and bring just to the boil. Take off the heat and add the butter and chocolate, broken into pieces. Leave to stand for a few minutes until the chocolate has melted, then stir until smooth. Leave to cool until the icing is thick enough to coat the back of a spoon. Use to decorate cakes while still warm.

mascarpone frosting

This is a great alternative to the icings mentioned on this page. Don't be scared to experiment with the icings on the cakes in this book – try this one first on some of the smaller individual cakes.

Beat 125 g (4 oz) mascarpone cheese in a bowl to soften, then mix in 175 g (6 oz) icing sugar and the grated rind of half a small orange. Don't overbeat, as the more you mix this icing, the softer it will become.

lemon cream

Covers Number Fun (see below or page 48).

200 ml (7 fl oz) double cream
2 tablespoons lemon curd

Lightly whip the cream until it forms soft peaks, then gently mix in the lemon curd. Spread the lemon cream over the cake and chill until ready to serve.

coloured icing

adding colour

Food colourings are available in two forms, paste and liquid. Paste colourings are much more intense and give a bold, vibrant effect when mixed into ready-to-roll and butter icings. A little goes a long way, so mix the paste colouring gradually into ready-to-roll icing or butter icing with the end of a cocktail stick. You will need slightly more colouring for ready-to-roll icing than for butter icing.

liquid colours

Liquid colours are ideal for pastel tones and are generally sold in supermarkets. Don't be tempted to keep adding colouring in the hope that the colour will intensify or you will end up with a sticky icing that is difficult to handle.

paste colours

Paste colours are available in small pots in a wide range of colours and tones from specialist cookshops or cake-decorating

▼ *This marbled icing finish gives an interesting and more realistic look to a fun cake.*

▲ *Knead paste or liquid colouring into ready-to-roll icing, either completely or partially for a marbled effect.*

shops. Some specialist shops also run a mail-order service. If you are starting from scratch, it is worth buying yellow, red, blue, green, black and brown, adding more unusual colours to your collection when you need them. Don't forget that tiny amounts of red colouring will make pink when mixed into icing, and, similarly, a little black can be used to make grey.

kneading icing

After adding the paste colouring, knead ready-to-roll icing well on a surface dusted with a little icing sugar or cornflour until it is evenly coloured, or knead briefly for an eye-catching, marbled effect, as in the Doyouthinkhesawus Dinosaur cake (see page 98).

Cornflour or icing sugar can be used when you are kneading or rolling out ready-to-roll icing, but cornflour is preferable if you are smoothing brightly coloured icing on a cake. It gives a good shine and is more readily absorbed, so that the true colour of the icing can be seen and is not masked by a fine dusting of white icing sugar.

storing

Once ready-to-roll icing has been coloured, it is important to keep it well wrapped so that it doesn't dry out or crack when rolled out. Store in clingfilm or small plastic bags and make sure to seal them well until you are ready to use.

painting colours

While colourings are mostly kneaded into ready-to-roll icing or stirred into softer icings, they can also be painted on to cakes.

Using a very fine brush, take out a little paste colouring and put it on to a saucer. Dilute it with a few drops of water and then paint on to a ready-to-roll iced cake, that has been allowed to dry (see the brick wall and sky for Humpty Dumpty on page 46, or the Eyeball Cake on page 116 for individually decorated cakes).

Colours may also be blended, just like ordinary paints in a palette. Make sure to wash the brush with cold water and dry it with kitchen paper before using another colour. If you are planning a multi-coloured cake, then allow one colour to dry before painting the next one, so they do not run and merge together. For large areas of single colour, you may find it easier to paint an outline and then fill in the shape.

Rice paper can also be painted with food colouring to make butterfly wings or boat sails. You could also use edible felt-tip pens, which are available from specialist cake-decorating shops. They can be used to write birthday messages directly on to dried icing, too.

▲ If you have a good cake-decorating supplier near you, then you can save time and buy coloured ready-to-roll icing in useful 250 g (8 oz) packs.

▼ Use a fine paintbrush to paint food colourings on to iced cakes.

QUICK TIPS

★ Food colourings can take a little while to develop to their full intensity, especially when using red or black. To help you see the true colour of the icing before using, knead in the colour, wrap the icing in clingfilm or a plastic bag and set aside for 5 minutes before use while you get out all the other equipment needed for the recipe.

★ A little paste food colouring goes a long way, so use it sparingly and take a little out of the pot on the end of a cocktail stick. It is better to build up the shade of colour gradually, rather than overdoing it at the beginning.

★ Use liquid colourings for making pastel coloured ready-to-roll or butter icings. Choose paste colours where a vibrant bold colour is needed, as these are more concentrated.

using ready-to-roll icing

making cake boards more fun

If you have time, it is fun to cover the cake board with a little plain, coloured or marbled ready-to-roll icing. This is also a great way of recycling old, battered boards. Spread a little smooth apricot jam over the cake board to act as glue. Roll out the ready-to-roll icing until fractionally larger than the board. Lift the icing over a rolling pin and then smooth it in place with your fingertips dusted with icing sugar or cornflour, or by using a special plastic smoother tool. Trim off any excess icing with a small knife.

▼ *Lift the rolled out icing with a rolling pin and cover a cake board to give a simple, decorative look.*

When trimming the edge, you may find it easier to hold the board with one hand and trim with the other in much the same way as trimming the edge of a pie. Alternatively, stand the cake board on top of a cake tin that is smaller than the size of the board. (An icing turntable may be used for this if you have one, but it is not essential.) Leave the icing to harden if you are not in too much of a hurry, then position the cake on the board and complete the decoration.

Butter icing or melted chocolate may also be spread around the finished cake to jazz up the cake board. Alternatively, spread it with a little jam and sprinkle with coloured desiccated coconut coloured with food colouring. For a quicker option, dust the board with sifted icing sugar, but make sure to shield the rest of the cake with a piece of paper first.

1

2

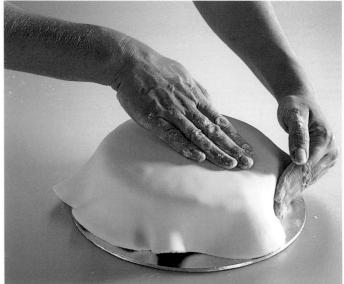

3

4

decorating cakes with ready-to-roll icing

With the wide availability of ready-to-roll icing, sometimes also known as fondant icing, even the most inexperienced cook can make an eye-catching and exciting birthday cake.

1 Spread the top and sides of the cake with smooth apricot jam or butter icing.

2 Knead the icing on a surface dusted with icing sugar or cornflour to soften it slightly, then roll it out. When the icing is almost the same size as the top and sides of the cake, lift it over a rolling pin and drape it over the cake.

3 Working quickly, smooth the icing in place over the top of the cake and down to the board with your fingertips dusted with icing sugar or cornflour .

4 When the icing is in place trim off the excess from the base of the cake. The cake is now ready to be decorated as you wish.

QUICK TIP

★ Some recipes recommend warming apricot jam with a little boiled water and then sieving it before use, but you can save time and effort if you buy smooth apricot jam or economy jam. Since it doesn't have any fruit pieces, the jam can be used straight from the jar. If it has a very set texture, warm it briefly in the microwave, still in the jar.

sweets and special touches

sweets, sweets and more sweets – lots to choose

All children love sweets – they're bright, colourful and an easy way to decorate cakes speedily. Buy them in large packs from the supermarket, from pick-and-mix sections in department stores or cinema foyers or from your local newsagent.

There's a wide range to choose from – here are the best:

★ Jelly beans, available in a wide range of bright colours and flavours and loved by kids of all ages. They are ideal to edge cakes or make facial features.

★ Candy-covered chocolates are also a timeless favourite and can now be bought in three sizes – jumbo, standard and mini, and in different colours. Make sure to put the logo side down when adding them to a cake. Again, these chocolates are perfect to edge cakes, to make wacky coloured eyes, or to use as spots on dominoes or as ship's portholes.

★ Chocolate buttons are always popular with very young children. Choose from white or milk chocolate or white with sugar sprinkles. They're great as eyes, ears, paws, paths, edging stones or roofing tiles.

▼ *Black jelly beans and clear boiled sweets complete this jewel-encrusted crown.*

▲ *Wrap any leftover sweets in squares of cellophane and decorate with curled ribbon and name tags – ideal to give away instead of party bags or to hang on a Christmas tree.*

★ Mini marshmallows, with their delicate pastel shades, lend themselves to pretty cakes and are perfect for edging around the top of a castle tower.

★ Liquorice sweets come in a variety of shapes, sizes and colours, from yellow and black, pink and black or white and black layered squares, to pink or blue sprinkled circles, to yellow and black, blue and black or pink and black sweets. Or choose from a range of all-black strips, twists, bars or squares. They are great for facial features or details on cars, trains or tanks. These sweets are a more adult taste so use in small amounts or for slightly older children.

★ Foil-wrapped chocolates – choose from gold- or silver-covered chocolate coins to mints or truffles or soft-centred toffee or fruit-filled chocolates wrapped in vibrant jewel-coloured foils. Use these as treasure, cargo, or even coal in a train truck.

★ Boiled, clear sweets – ideal for paints, windows or jewels. Stick sweets in place if needed with a generous blob of piping icing. Don't add until the very last minute as the moisture from the cake icing can cause the sweets to dissolve.

★ Bootlaces – these long, thin string-like sweets were traditionally made with liquorice, but are now available in strawberry and apple flavours too. Twist and add to cakes as hair, to mark the edges of a cake, as in the Dominoes (see page 54) or as a smile on any iced face. Keep any leftover sweets wrapped in clingfilm as they quickly dry out.

what about special diets?

If catering for vegetarian children check packs of sweets carefully. Brightly coloured red sweets are nearly always coloured with an animal-based product, so beware of E120 or cochineal, made from crushed insects. E124 Ponceau 4R is acceptable and sometimes known as Cochineal Red A, or E162 can also be included as it is made of beetroot juice.

Jellied sweets may contain gelatine; choose those with guar gum instead. Milk chocolate coatings on sweets may contain animal-based emulsifiers which may not be listed on the packs. Look out for the V-shaped vegetarian approved symbol if in doubt.

Brightly coloured sweets may also be a problem if you have a hyperactive child. Again, check the back of packs for listed ingredients and avoid any E numbers, artificial colourings and flavourings. Many larger supermarkets now sell natural-coloured candy-covered chocolate sweets, so it's worth looking around.

choosing candles

A child's birthday cake wouldn't be complete without candles. Look for dotty, glittery, striped, tall, short or wiggly candles. What about novelty Halloween or Christmas candles too? There are even candles that play a tune or ones that keep relighting when they are blown out just to add to the fun.

Make sure you put candles in holders to catch any melting wax. Alternatively, make your own candle-holders with tiny balls or shapes of ready-to-roll icing.

► *Think carefully about the positioning of candles on a cake, so they do not spoil the cake design.*

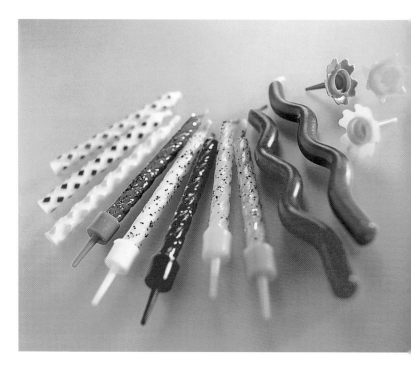

▲ *Choose coloured candles to match or complement the look and colour of the cake.*

the cakes

dot-to-dot

Serves 16 children
Decoration time: 15 minutes

2 x 100 g (3½ oz) packs strawberry poles or liquorice strips
2 packs candy-covered chocolate drops
23 cm (9 inch) round bought or home-made Madeira Cake
   (see page 20)
25 cm (10 inch) thin round silver cake board
single quantity White Chocolate Fudge Frosting
   (see page 24)
candles and candle-holders (optional)

1 Design a dot-to-dot shape on a plate the same size as the cake top, snipping strawberry poles or liquorice strips into the desired lengths and choosing favourite-coloured candy-covered chocolate drops for dots.

2 Put the cake on the cake board and quickly spread the top and sides with a thin layer of warm white chocolate fudge frosting to stick the crumbs in place, then spoon on the remaining frosting and smooth with a palette knife.

3 Press the sweets on to the cake top. Cut leftover strawberry poles or liquorice strips into 2.5 cm (1 inch) strips and press them on to the sides in a zig-zag pattern, adding candy-covered chocolate drops in between. Add candles and candle-holders, if you like, then leave to stand for 15 minutes or longer for the frosting to harden.

► *Work out the design of the sweets on a plate the same size as the top of the cake. You may like to make a design that your child loves in a favourite bedtime story book or colouring book.*

QUICK TIPS

★ The cake could also be covered with Dark Chocolate Fudge Frosting (see page 25) or flavoured Butter Icing (see page 23).

★ If the frosting begins to set before you have finished smoothing out any thick knife lines, warm the palette knife in boiling water and continue.

★ Experiment with different designs – you could also write a child's name around the side of the cake with mini candy-covered chocolate drops and strawberry bootlaces.

chocolate box

Serves 4–5 children
Decoration time: 10 minutes

100 g (3½ oz) pack white chocolate drops
15 cm (6 inch) bought or home-made filled Victoria
    Sandwich Cake (see page 19)
18 cm (7 inch) thin round silver cake board
200 g (7 oz) assorted foil-covered chocolates
pink paste food colouring
pink organza ribbon

1 Set a heatproof bowl over a small saucepan half filled with water. Bring the water to the boil, then remove from the heat and add the chocolate drops to the bowl. Leave until melted.

2 Cut a strip of nonstick baking paper a little wider than the depth of the cake and long enough to wrap around the cake. Cut a second, square piece and draw a heart shape on it a little smaller than the top of the cake. Arrange half of the sweets on top of the cake.

3 Stir the melted chocolate and spoon it over the baking paper strip and inside the drawn heart. Dot randomly with a little food colouring, then spread with a palette knife for a marbled effect over the heart shape until the strip is thickly covered.

4 Carefully lift the paper strip and press the melted chocolate side on to the side of the cake so that the paper is on the outside. Chill the cake and heart shape for at least 15 minutes, until set.

5 Carefully peel the baking paper away from the chocolate. Arrange the remaining sweets on top of the cake and lay the heart on top of the sweets. Complete with a ribbon tied around the side of the cake.

▲ *Nonstick baking paper peels easily away from the chilled chocolate strip to give this simple but eye-catching finish.*

QUICK TIPS

★ For chocolate enthusiasts, use a chocolate cake with a chocolate filling.

★ If you are making this cake at the last minute, don't forget to allow time for the chocolate to set before serving.

★ You can use dark chocolate and leave it plain, or a mixture of white and dark chocolate for a bolder marbled effect.

★ For Valentine's day, cut a larger round cake into a heart shape and then wrap with chocolate or red ready-to-roll icing.

paintbox cake

Serves 6 children
Decoration time: 20 minutes

275 g (9 oz) bought or home-made Madeira (see page 20)
    or bought angel cake
20 cm (8 inch) thin square silver cake board
2 tablespoons smooth apricot jam
200 g (7 oz) white ready-to-roll icing
icing sugar or cornflour, for dusting
125 g (4 oz) red ready-to-roll icing
black paste food colouring
5 different-coloured clear fruit sweets or jelly sweets
selection of crayon candles

1 Cut the cake in half lengthways and put both pieces on the cake board at a slight angle with the long edges touching. Spread the top and sides of each half with jam.

2 Knead and roll out three-quarters of the white icing on a surface lightly dusted with icing sugar or cornflour. Wrap the remaining icing in clingfilm.

3 Drape the rolled-out white icing over the cakes, form a ridge around the edge and make a cavity for the brush holder and paints. Smooth over the sides and trim off the excess. Knead any trimmings again.

4 Reserve half of the red icing to make the paintbrush. Knead and shape the remainder into a rope long enough to go around the paintbox base and lid. Flatten with a rolling pin and cut into a thin strip with a pastry wheel. Stick it around the base of the paintbox with water.

5 Shape the reserved red icing into a paintbrush handle. Use some of the white trimmings to make the 'ferrule'. Colour a little of the remaining white icing black and roll out into a strip. Make a series of cuts almost down to the base, like a fringe, then roll up for brush bristles. Press the bristles on to the ferrule. Place the brush in the paintbox and arrange the sweets to resemble paints. Insert the appropriate number of crayon candles into balls of white icing and stick them on to the cake board. Arrange the remaining candles on the lid of the paintbox.

QUICK TIPS

★ For very young children, use soft jelly sweets rather than hard, boiled sweets.

★ Although the cake may be made several days in advance, don't add the sweets until just before the party, as they will begin to dissolve after a few hours.

◀ *Form a ridge around the edges of the cake to make an area for the 'paints' to sit on.*

funny faces

Serves 12 children
Decoration time: 20 minutes

**75 g (3 oz) luxury dark cooking chocolate, broken
   into pieces**
12 bought or home-made Fairy Cakes (see page 19)
single quantity Butter Icing (see page 23)
pink or brown paste food colouring
selection of mini candy-covered chocolate drops
1 tube red writing icing
few sugar flowers (optional)

1 Set a heatproof bowl over a small saucepan of water. Bring the water to the boil, then remove from the heat. Add the chocolate to the bowl and leave for 2–3 minutes, until melted.

2 If the cakes are very domed, trim slightly to level them. Colour the butter icing to a skin tone, then spread it over the tops of the cakes.

3 Add sweets for eyes and pipe on red mouths. Stir the chocolate and spoon it into a greaseproof paper piping bag (see below). Snip off the tip and pipe on hair, glasses and eye details. Add sugar flowers to the girls' hair styles, if you like, then leave the cakes in a cool place until the chocolate has set.

QUICK TIP

★ Coloured tubes of writing icing may be used for hair instead of the melted chocolate.

▲ *Make these little cakes multi-racial by colouring the butter icing with pink food colouring, melted chocolate or brown food colouring.*

BE IMAGINATIVE
Use the ideas here as a starting point to add a more personal touch and decorate the cakes to look like the members of your family or your child's friends. If you have time to spare, shape ready-to-roll icing hats, scarves, bow ties or even arms and legs. For children suffering with chicken pox or some other illness, it may be fun to pipe on red spots to help cheer them up.

snakes and ladders

Serves 12 children
Decoration time: 25 minutes

3 bought Battenberg cakes
25 cm (10 inch) thin square cake board
1 tablespoon smooth apricot jam
2 lattice-shaped chocolate bars
200 g (7 oz) white ready-to-roll icing
red, yellow and green paste food colourings
icing sugar or cornflour, for dusting
1 tube red writing icing
1 tube yellow writing icing
few edible silver balls
6 different-coloured candy-covered chocolate drops
candles and candle-holders

1 Cut the marzipan covering away from the cakes and reserve. Thickly slice the cakes and place the slices close together on the cake board, arranging them so that the colours alternate to give a chequerboard effect.

2 Cut the reserved marzipan into strips the same thickness as the cake. Brush the edges of the cake with jam and cover the sides with the marzipan strips. Unwrap the chocolate bars, cut

▼ *Use tubes of brightly coloured writing icing to pipe patterns on the snakes.*

them into different lengths and arrange the pieces at angles on the cake to make ladders.

3 Colour a small ball of white ready-to-roll icing red on a surface lightly dusted with icing sugar or cornflour, then cut it into a cube for one of the dice. Cut the remaining icing in half. Colour half orange with a little red and yellow colouring, and the rest green. Shape a cube of green icing for the second die in the same way as the red one and set aside.

4 On a surface lightly dusted with icing sugar or cornflour, roll some of the remaining green icing into a rope, shape into a small snake, then lift on to the cake. Make a second, larger orange snake and then an orange and green snake by twisting two ropes of coloured icing together and curving them into a snake shape. Roll out the green trimmings and use to make a small arrow. Place the arrow on the bottom left-hand corner of the cake to mark the start of the game.

5 Decorate the snakes with zig-zag lines of red and yellow writing icing. Stick silver ball 'eyes' on the snakes with a little yellow icing, then pipe yellow dots on the dice. Arrange the dice and coloured sweet counters on the cake. Complete with candles to mark the end of the game.

QUICK TIPS

★ If you can't get lattice-shaped chocolate bars for the ladders, use chocolate sticks with smaller pieces for rungs. Alternatively, make the ladders with strips of brown ready-to-roll icing.

★ For avid marzipan fans, simply slice the cake and arrange on the board without removing the marzipan first.

GREAT FOR GRANDPARENTS TOO
For grandparents or parents it would be fun to make up the board with the same number of sponge cake squares as their age. Pipe on tiny numbers and then add a large birthday number at the finish.

* Many children find the taste of marzipan too strong and that is why it has been used to edge only the sides of the cake. Alternatively, use pink, yellow and white layered angel cake and cut into 3 long strips before slicing. Arrange individual squares of the cake on the board and edge the cake with yellow ready-to-roll icing instead.

funny clown

Serves 8 children
Decoration time: 20 minutes

18 cm (7 inch) bought or home-made Victoria
   Sandwich Cake (see page 19)
single quantity vanilla Butter Icing (see page 23)
23 cm (9 inch) thin round cake board
500 g (1 lb) white ready-to-roll icing
icing sugar or cornflour, for dusting
125 g (4 oz) red ready-to-roll icing
125 g (4 oz) blue ready-to-roll icing
1 yellow and black liquorice sweet
100 g (3½ oz) apple- or strawberry-flavoured
   bootlaces
1 tube green or red writing icing

1 Sandwich the two halves of the cake layer together with a thick layer of the vanilla butter icing. Place them on the cake board and then spread the top and sides of the cake and the rim of the board thinly with the butter icing as well. Reserve the remaining butter icing.

2 Knead the white ready-to-roll icing, then roll it out on a surface that is lightly dusted with icing sugar or cornflour until it is large enough to cover the entire cake and rim of the board. Lift the icing by draping it over the rolling pin, smooth it over the cake with your fingertips dusted with icing sugar or cornflour and press it over the cake board so that it is firmly in place. Trim off the excess with a knife.

3 Shape a ball for the clown's nose and a rope about 12 cm (5 inches) long from the red ready-to-roll icing. Curve the rope and flatten with a rolling pin for the mouth. Transfer the nose and mouth to the top of the cake, sticking them in place with a little of the remaining butter icing.

4 Knead the blue ready-to-roll icing, roll out thinly on a surface lightly dusted with icing sugar or cornflour and cut out a 28 x 6 cm (11 x 2½ inch) rectangle. Place this on the base of the cake in a wavy line, sticking it in place with dots of butter icing. Re-roll the trimmings and cut 2 eyes and a thin strip for the centre of the mouth. Press these on to the cake.

▲ *Make the bootlaces curly by wrapping them around the handle of a wooden spoon or metal skewer, hold for 1–2 minutes, then slide off and stick on to the cake for clown hair.*

5 Halve the liquorice sweet and stick it on to the cake for eyeballs. For the hair, twist the bootlaces around a wooden spoon handle or metal skewer, hold for 1–2 minutes, then slide off and stick them on to the cake with writing icing.

QUICK TIPS

★ If you can't buy ready-coloured ready-to-roll icing, then colour your own using paste food colouring. Liquid colours do not give the same intensity and too much will make the icing sticky and watery.

★ For children who don't like liquorice, make the eyeballs with two small balls of leftover white icing.

★ Icing sugar or cornflour helps stop icing sticking to a work surface and is good to smooth and polish icing when on the cake. Cornflour is better when working with dark reds and blues as it disappears as you smooth, while icing sugar may leave a faint white mark.

humpty dumpty

Serves 8 children
Decoration time: 30 minutes

**18 cm (7 inch) bought or home-made chocolate Victoria
     Sandwich Cake (see page 19)**
single quantity vanilla Butter Icing (see page 23)
35 x 25 cm (14 x 10 inch) thin cake board
6 bought mini chocolate Swiss rolls
250 g (8 oz) yellow ready-to-roll icing
icing sugar or cornflour, for dusting
375 g (12 oz) red ready-to-roll icing
75 g (3 oz) black ready-to-roll icing
550 g (1 lb 2 oz) white ready-to-roll icing
2 candles
few strawberry-flavoured bootlaces

1 Cut the cake layers into an oval shape and sandwich together with butter icing. Spread butter icing thinly over the top and sides of the cake, reserving about 1 tablespoon. Carefully transfer the cake to the cake board, positioning it closer to the top than the bottom.

2 To make the arms, cut a diagonal slice off two Swiss rolls so that they fit at an angle to the cake body. Trim a third off two more Swiss rolls and reserve for boots.

3 Knead the yellow icing and roll out on a surface lightly dusted with icing sugar or cornflour to an 18 x 13 cm (7 x 5½ inch) rectangle. Drape the rectangle over the top half of Humpty's body and smooth over the surface with your fingertips dusted with cornflour. Trim off the excess icing and reserve.

4 Knead and roll out two-thirds of the red icing and cover the other half of Humpty's body in the same way. Re-roll the trimmings and cut a trouser belt about 1.5 cm (¾ inch) wide, press on to the cake, adding two triangles and a strip for the bow.

5 Knead and roll out the remaining red icing and any trimmings, cut it into pieces and use to cover the arms and legs, sticking it in place with a little butter icing and pressing the edges over the ends of the Swiss rolls. (Use the diagonally trimmed Swiss rolls

▲ *Shape two balls of white ready-to-roll icing into a mitten shape, then cut slits to make fingers and thumbs. Shape the hands around the candles, then attach them to the cake arms with pieces of plastic drinking straw or wooden or plastic cocktail sticks.*

for arms and the uncut Swiss rolls for legs.) Position them next to the body and shape a mouth from the trimmings.

6 Roll out the yellow trimmings and cut 1.5 cm (¾ inch) circles using a small biscuit cutter or upturned piping tube for the dots on the trousers. Stick on to the cake with a little butter icing.

7 Knead and roll out the black icing and cover the boots in the same way as the legs. Roll out 50 g (2 oz) of the white icing, cut two strips and wrap them around the legs for socks. Shape two white ovals for eyes and stick them on to the cake. Shape two larger balls for hands, flatten, then slit to make fingers. Wrap the fingers around a candle and attach the hands to the cake with a little butter icing or use 2 pieces of plastic drinking straw or two halved cocktail sticks per hand. Complete the cake with two small black icing rounds for eyeballs and bootlace hair.

8 Roll our the remaining white icing and cover the board. Add a strip across the board for the top of the wall. Place the iced cake on the board and paint on brown bricks with a fine paintbrish and a little food colouring, diluted with a few drops of water. Brush on blue sky in the same way, leaving gaps for clouds.

★ If you are very short of time, leave the trousers one colour, omitting the yellow dots, or stick on different-coloured candy-covered chocolate drops.

number fun

Serves 10 children
Decoration time: 20 minutes

2 x 275 g (9 oz) bought or home-made Madeira cakes
 (see page 20)
6 tablespoons smooth strawberry jam
20 cm (8 inch) square silver cake board
single quantity Lemon Cream (see page 25)
selection of candles and candle-holders
75 g (3 oz) each red, yellow and green ready-to-roll icing
icing sugar or cornflour, for dusting

1 Cut each cake in half lengthways and sandwich the pieces together with strawberry jam. Place the cake diagonally on the board so that the jam stripes are vertical.

2 Spread the top and sides of the cake with the lemon cream, then add candle-holders and candles.

3 Roll out each colour of ready-to-roll icing separately on a surface lightly dusted with icing sugar or cornflour and stamp out numbers using small biscuit cutters. Press the numbers on to the cake and cake board, then chill until ready to serve.

SPONGE EFFECTS
To make the cake even more eye-catching, you could use one plain and one chocolate cake and butt alternate coloured slices of cake together. If you want to go a stage further, split the cakes crossways and arrange the cubes in a chequerboard pattern.

► *Cut bought Madeira cakes into slices and then sandwich them together with jam so that the layers run vertically instead of the more usual horizontal layers.*

QUICK TIPS

★ The cake could also be spread with Mascarpone Frosting (see page 25) or double quantity vanilla or plain Butter Icing (see page 23).

★ For chocolate fans, sandwich and decorate with chocolate Butter Icing (see page 23) or Chocolate Fudge Frosting (see pages 24–25) and add bought chocolate letters or numbers cut from melted chocolate spread over nonstick baking paper.

★ If you are very short of time, press candy-covered chocolate drops randomly over the cake for a spotty or rainbow cake.

★ A home-made 18 cm (7 inch) square Victoria Sandwich Cake (see page 18) could also be split and decorated in the same way.

two today

Serves 12–14 children
Decoration time: 20 minutes

3 x 18 cm (7 inch) bought chocolate Swiss rolls
33 x 23 cm (13 x 9 inch) thin red foil cake board
double quantity of chocolate Butter Icing (see page 23)
200 g (7 oz) jelly beans
75 g (3 oz) milk chocolate buttons
75 g (3 oz) white chocolate buttons
2 packs candy-covered chocolate drops
20 candy cones
candles and candle-holders (optional)

1 Place one of the Swiss rolls along the shortest side of the cake board to make the base of the number. Cut a small diagonal slice off the end of the second Swiss roll and position the long piece on the board with the cut surface against the left

❚ *Cut three triangular slices from one Swiss roll, and just one slice from the second. Leave the third Swiss roll uncut.*

↖ *Arrange the uncut Swiss roll as the base of the number, use the next longest one as the diagonal line and use the sliced Swiss roll to make the curved top.*

end of the first Swiss roll. To make the curve at the top of the number, you will need to use trimmed slices of Swiss roll turned around. Cut the remaining Swiss roll into four pieces – two small triangular slices off opposing ends and then two large pieces from what is left. Turn these pieces around where appropriate and position them on the board to make the correct shape.

2 Stick the cakes in place with a little butter icing, then spread the remainder over the top and sides, smoothing it with a palette or round-bladed knife.

3 Arrange a border of jelly beans all around the number, then fill in the shape using rows of different sweets, including milk and white chocolate buttons, candy-covered chocolate drops and candy cones. Add candles and candle-holders if you like.

WHAT ABOUT OTHER NUMBERS?
Adapt this idea to make other numerals, such as 1, 3, 4 and 5. For 6, 8 and 9, use one or two 15 cm (6 inch) filled Victoria Sandwich Cakes (see page 18) and cut out the centre of the cakes with a plain round biscuit cutter or upturned glass.

★ Keep the cake in the refrigerator if the weather is very hot.

★ You could also use White Chocolate Fudge Frosting (see page 24) or Mascarpone Icing (see page 25).

what's the time?

Serves 10 children
Decoration time: 30 minutes

3 tablespoons smooth apricot jam
10 bought chocolate Bourbon or chocolate bar biscuits
**   (without icing)**
150 g (5 oz) white ready-to-roll icing
150 g (5 oz) yellow ready-to-roll icing
150 g (5 oz) red ready-to-roll icing
icing sugar or cornflour, for dusting
10 round glazed spiced biscuits
1 tube red writing icing

1 Spread the jam thinly over the chocolate biscuits and place them on a tray lined with nonstick baking paper or waxed paper.

2 Knead each of the coloured ready-to-roll icings separately on a surface dusted with icing sugar or cornflour until softened. Roll out each piece to a 20 x 12 cm (8 x 5 inch) rectangle on a surface dusted with icing sugar or cornflour.

3 Cut each colour into long thin strips about 5 mm (¼ inch) wide. Butt alternate strips together to form 3 striped rectangles of icing , each about 20 x 12 cm (8 x 5 inches). Flatten them with a rolling pin so that the stripes stick together, then cut into 5 cm (2 inch) wide strips.

4 Working quickly, lift the icing strips with a palette knife and drape them over the chocolate biscuits, smooth the surface with sugared fingers and trim the icing if necessary. Mark holes on the straps with the end of a skewer.

5 Stick round glazed biscuits on the straps with jam, then pipe on red numbers for the watch faces and red buckles. Shape tiny yellow hands from icing trimmings and pipe a red dot in the centre of each. Leave to set, then serve.

► *To make the striking watch straps, butt strips of coloured icing together, then roll out so that they stick together.*

THINK BIG
A large clock cake could be made with a Victoria Sandwich Cake (see page 19) filled and topped with Butter Icing (see page 23). Decorate with coloured ready-to-roll icing numbers stamped out with tiny biscuit number cutters and ready-to-roll icing hands.

QUICK TIPS

★ Ready-coloured icing is available from any good cake-decorating supplier, but if you don't have one near you then you will need to colour packs of white ready-to-roll icing from the supermarket with paste colours.

★ If you are very short of time, make the straps one colour and the buckles a different one.

★ Watch faces could also be made with chocolate-covered marshmallows.

dominoes

Makes 18
Decoration time: 20 minutes

30 x 23 x 5 cm (12 x 9 x 2 inch) plain or orange-flavoured traybake Madeira Cake (see page 20)
double quantity vanilla- or orange-flavoured Butter Icing (see page 23)
2 tubes candy-covered chocolate drops
50 g (2 oz) strawberry-flavoured bootlaces

1 With the longest edge of the cake nearest you, cut it into 3 x 7 cm (3 inch) wide bars, and then cut each into 6 small bars.

2 Spread butter icing over the top of the cakes and then decorate with groups of coloured sweets to resemble domino dots. Separate the 2 sets of dots with a strip of bootlace and then press lengths of bootlace around the edges of the cakes to make borders. Arrange on a plate or cake board and serve.

QUICK TIPS

★ Plain uncut cake can be frozen and then decorated with butter icing and frozen without the sweets. Alternatively, use bought cake bars. These are ideal if you have only a couple of children for tea, as they are so quick to defrost.

★ You could also make the cakes into mini sums by stamping out numbers, crosses for addition and multiplication, single strips for subtraction and double strips for the equals signs.

★ Dominoes could also be made from slices of bought Madeira cake or trimmed trifle sponges.

WHAT'S YOUR NAME?
Cut and butter-ice the cakes as for the Dominoes, but instead of decorating them with sweets pipe on the names of your child's friends with melted dark chocolate or tubes of coloured writing icing.

◄ *All children love candy-covered chocolate drops, so make sure you keep them hidden away until you're ready to use them.*

building bricks

Serves 9 children
Decoration time: 30 minutes

20 cm (8 inch) square home-made plain or flavoured
  Madeira Cake (see page 20)
double quantity plain Butter Icing (see page 23)
500 g (1 lb) red ready-to-roll icing
icing sugar or cornflour, for dusting
500 g (1 lb) blue ready-to-roll icing
500 g (1 lb) yellow ready-to-roll icing
2 packs candy-coated chocolate drops
1 tube yellow writing icing
1 tube red writing icing
candles and candle-holders (optional)

1 If necessary, level the surface of the cake and then cut it into 9 even-sized blocks.

2 Spread the tops and sides of the cake blocks thinly with butter icing, leaving the bases plain.

3 Lightly knead the red icing, then roll it out thinly on a surface lightly dusted with icing sugar or cornflour to a 38 x 20 cm (15 x 8 inch) rectangle. Cut it into 15 squares, then stick them on to the cakes. Repeat with the blue, then the yellow icing, until all the butter-iced sides of the cakes are covered.

4 Stick sweets around the edges of the cakes with writing icing, then pipe letters or numbers. Stack the cakes on a cake board, adding candles to the tops of some of the cakes, if you like.

► *Help speed up the decorating time by cutting the icing into a grid and sticking squares of icing from the grid on to the cakes before rolling out a second or third colour.*

QUICK TIPS

★ Larger packs of ready-coloured ready-to-roll icing can be bought from specialist cake-decorating shops. If you don't have one near you, colour plain white icing with paste food colourings instead.

★ Slices of bought Madeira cake can be used instead of homemade cake. Buy three cakes, cut a slice off the top of each to level and then cut each into 3 pieces.

★ For very little children, the bricks could be cut smaller, making 16 instead, but do allow extra time as they will be more fiddly to ice.

★ If you prefer cakes with a little less fondant icing, then press coloured sugar strands and grated white or dark chocolate on to the sides and just add rolled-out icing to the front and top of the cubes.

mini racers

Serves 12 children
Decoration time: 15 minutes

12 bought or home-made Fairy Cakes (see page 18)
single quantity green Butter Icing (see page 23)
150 g (5 oz) grey ready-to-roll icing
icing sugar or cornflour, for dusting
1 tube white writing icing
12 micro machine cars
12 mini flags

1 Trim the tops of the cakes to level them, if necessary. Spread the tops with butter icing.

2 Knead the grey icing and roll it out on a surface lightly dusted with icing sugar or cornflour. Stamp out 6 cm (2½ inch) circles using a plain biscuit cutter, then cut out a small circle from the centre of each with a 2.5 cm (1 inch) cutter. Arrange the circles on the cakes. You will need 12 circles, so re-roll the trimmings and cut more, if necessary.

3 Pipe on road markings with white writing icing. Add the cars and flags and arrange on a plate or cake board. Remove non-edible decorations before eating, and be especially careful when giving to young children.

QUICK TIPS

★ Tiny micro machine cars are sold in all good toy shops and can sometimes be bought in bargain stores in packs of 3 or 4 cars. Alternatively, raid your child's playroom and wash the cars before using.

★ If you don't have any plain biscuit cutters, use fluted biscuit cutters the other way up or use a glass and a bottle cap as a guide instead.

★ If you can't buy ready-coloured grey icing, then knead a little black paste colouring into some plain white icing.

▲ *Roll out grey ready-to-roll icing and cut a car track using two plain round cutters, one smaller than the other.*

tip-up truck

Serves 10 children
Decoration time: 30 minutes

3 x 275 g (9 oz) bought or home-made Madeira cakes
    (see page 20)
single quantity chocolate Butter Icing (see page 23)
23 x 10 cm (9 x 4 inch) thin silver cake board
500 g (1 lb) orange ready-to-roll icing
icing sugar or cornflour, for dusting
250 g (8 oz) brown ready-to-roll icing
selection of liquorice sweets
1 tube yellow writing icing
2 x 200 g (7 oz) clean, dry sweetcorn, baked bean or
    spaghetti hoop cans, labels removed
4 chocolate-covered marshmallow-filled biscuits or other
    chocolate-covered biscuits, the same size as the cans
4 blue flying-saucer sweets
20 g (¾ oz) pack edible silver balls
selection foil-wrapped sweets
candles and candle-holders (optional)

▲ *To make the wheel detail, stick a flying-saucer sweet on to the centre of each chocolate biscuit, then decorate with edible silver balls stuck on to small dots of yellow icing piped around the edge of the sweets to make hub caps.*

1 Cut one of the cakes in half crossways and sandwich the pieces on top of each other with chocolate butter icing for the truck cab. Spread more butter icing thinly over the top and sides.

2 Knead the orange ready-to-roll icing and cut off one-third. Wrap the remainder. Roll out the smaller piece on a surface lightly dusted with icing sugar or cornflour. Cut a long piece to go over the top and sides of the cab, then pieces for the front and back. Press in place. Put on one end of the cake board.

3 Sandwich the remaining cakes together with butter icing along their longest sides and butt up against the truck cab to make the tip-up container. Spread three-quarters of the remaining butter icing over the top and sides of the container.

4 Roll out some of the brown ready-to-roll icing and cover the bottom third of the truck. Re-roll some of the trimmings and cut a brown bumper and mudguards. Stick them on to the cab.

5 Roll out the remaining orange icing, cut a strip and use to line the inside of the tip-up container. Cut an 18 x 7 cm (7 x 3 inch) rectangle. Cut in half diagonally, then place the triangles on either side of the truck so that they come to the roof of the cab and just above the tip-up container lining. Use the trimmings to make a roof and door for the cab. Mark the roof with a ruler.

6 Stick liquorice sweets on to the cab with yellow writing icing for windows and lights. Put a little of the remaining ready-to-roll icing on the cans to stop them rolling around and place them, on their sides, on a cake board. Stand the truck – on its board – on top of the cans. Stick flying-saucer sweets on to the chocolate biscuits using yellow writing icing, then use icing to stick on silver balls to decorate the 'hub caps'. Stick the biscuits on to the cans with some of the remaining chocolate butter icing. Complete with sweets and candles.

QUICK TIPS

✱ If using a home-made cake, you will need a 15 cm (6 inch) square cake. Cut off one-third to make the truck cab.

✱ If you can't obtain a narrow cake board, cover a piece of cardboard or a double thickness piece of cereal packet with foil.

pirate ship

Serves 16 children
Decoration time: 30 minutes

4 x 300 g (10 oz) bought double chocolate loaf cakes
35 x 20 cm (14 x 8 inch) thin silver cake board
double quantity chocolate Butter Icing (see page 23)
2 x 150 g (5 oz) packs chocolate finger biscuits
8 giant candy-covered chocolate drops
7 long wooden skewers
raffia or fine string
selection of orange, green and black paper
sticky tape
selection of small plastic pirate figures
shredded blue tissue paper

▼ *To make the paper sails, pierce the top with a hole punch and tie to wooden skewer masts with raffia or fine string.*

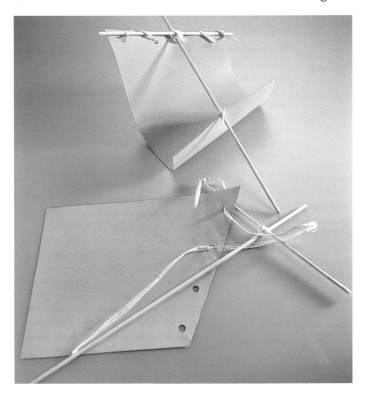

1 Level the tops of the cakes, if necessary. Put two cakes on the cake board and sandwich the two shortest sides together with a little butter icing. Cut one-third off one of the cakes. Spread the top of the cakes with butter icing and stick the other two cakes on top with the small slice in the centre so that the second layer extends over the first. Cut one end to a point for the prow of the ship and put one of the off-cuts underneath to support it.

2 Spread the remaining butter icing over the top and sides of the cake, then stick chocolate fingers over both sides and add candy-covered chocolate drops for portholes.

3 To make the masts, tie two skewers in a cross shape with a little raffia or string and trim the sticks, if necessary. Repeat to make 2 more. Cut rectangles of paper for sails, make holes along the top edge with a hole punch and lace to the masts with raffia or string. Add a hole to the centre base of the sails and tie down to the masts. Add a triangular sail to a single stick mast. Cut black flags and tape to the top of the masts, then insert into the cake.

4 Complete the cake with plastic pirate figures and tissue paper sea arranged on the cake board.

QUICK TIPS

★ If you are unable to find chocolate loaf cakes the same size as required in the recipe, buy whatever is available and increase or reduce the quantity of icing and the number of finger biscuits accordingly. Some loaf cakes can be very domed, so level the tops before using.

★ The cake board could also be covered with a sea of blue butter icing or desiccated coconut, coloured blue and stuck in place with a little jam.

battle tank

Serves: 16 children
Decoration time: 30 minutes

2 x 275 g (9 oz) bought or home-made Madeira Cakes (see page 20) or angel cakes
double quantity dark green Butter Icing (see page 23)
30 cm (12 inch) thin round silver cake board
2 x 23 cm (9 inch) jumbo chocolate or jam Swiss rolls
1 round chocolate-covered marshmallow-filled biscuit
plastic soldiers (optional)
brown paste food colouring
1 wooden skewer
12 liquorice Catherine wheels
mixed coloured liquorice sweets
1 liquorice bar

1 Sandwich the long sides of the Madeira cakes together with a little butter icing and place in the centre of the cake board. Cut a sloping slice off the end for the front of the tank.

2 Cut a 4 cm (1½ inch) slice off the end of each Swiss roll. Reserve one slice for the gun turret. Cut the other slice in half, crossways, reserving one of the thinner slices for the turret lid and discarding (or eating) the other. Position the larger sections of the Swiss rolls either side of the tank body and stick in place with a little butter icing. Cut a little off the top of each end so that they slope for wheels.

3 Stick the biscuit and the larger slice of Swiss roll on to the tank body for the gun turret and add a soldier, if you like.

4 Colour 2 tablespoons of the butter icing brown. Cover the tank thinly with green butter icing, then add a second, thicker layer, incorporating the brown icing randomly. Spread to give a camouflage effect. Cover the thin Swiss roll slice with butter icing and rest it on the turret with a wooden skewer for support.

5 Stick 8 liquorice Catherine wheels on to the sides of the tank. Unwind the remaining Catherine wheels and snip the liquorice into pieces. Press the pieces on to the Swiss rolls for tracks and use to add details to the gun turret. Add extra sweets to the tank body for detail. Trim the liquorice bar and add to the turret for the gun, supporting it with the trimmed piece.

▲ *There's no cooking with this cake – simply use two bought Madeira or angel cakes for the tank body, plus two chocolate Swiss rolls for the tracks and gun turret, adding a little extra height to the gun turret with a large chocolate biscuit.*

6 Colour the remaining butter icing dark brown and spread it thinly over the cake board. Add extra plastic soldiers if you like.

QUICK TIPS

★ Substitute 2 plain digestive biscuits for the chocolate biscuit, if you like.

★ If the liquorice gun seems to droop, shorten the liquorice bar or prop it up with a cocktail stick, but remember to remove it before serving.

★ For children who hate liquorice, use mini chocolate digestive biscuits instead of Catherine wheels and single squares of chocolate for the wheel decoration, a chocolate finger biscuit for the gun and jelly or chocolate sweets for extra detail.

space rocket

Serves 6 children
Decoration time: 30 minutes

1 kg (2 lb) white ready-to-roll icing
icing sugar or cornflour, for dusting
black paste food colouring
30 cm (12 inch) thin round cake board
3 tablespoons smooth apricot jam
1 ice cream cone
350 g (11½ oz) bought chocolate marble cake
6 chocolate mini Swiss rolls
6 strawberry twists
1 tube red writing icing
2 flat liquorice bootlaces
few black and white square and tube-shaped liquorice
    sweets
few edible silver balls
silver, red or white candles and candle-holders

1 Knead half of the white ready-to-roll icing on a surface lightly dusted with icing sugar or cornflour. Knead in some black paste food colouring, but don't worry about mixing it in fully. Keep the remaining white icing wrapped in clingfilm so that it doesn't dry out.

2 Tear off some of the grey icing, shape into rings and balls and press on to the cake board to make a lunar landscape. Brush the edges of the board with a little jam. Roll out the remaining grey icing, drape it over the cake board and smooth it into place. Trim off the excess.

3 Trim the bottom end off the ice cream cone and stick the 'nose cone' to the end of the marble cake with jam. Spread the remaining jam over the top and sides of the cake and use to stick the mini rolls together in a pyramid-style stack, with three mini rolls on the bottom, then two and then one.

4 Roll out two-thirds of the reserved white icing and drape it over the marble cake and nose cone. Smooth it into place with your fingertips dusted with icing sugar. Trim off the excess and press the edges together well under the cone. Place on the cake board. Cover the stack of mini rolls with the remaining icing rolled into a strip the same width as the mini rolls. Smooth it over

▲ *Cover a stack of mini chocolate Swiss rolls with a rectangular piece of ready-to-roll white icing to make rocket engines.*

the mini rolls, then trim off the excess. Carefully place it next to the rocket body.

5 Halve three strawberry twists by cutting with scissors and stick them on to the rocket engine with writing icing. Add pieces to the body of the rocket too. Snip the flat liquorice bootlaces to the right length with scissors and stick on to the nose cone and body of the rocket with writing icing.

6 Thinly slice the black and white liquorice sweets and stick them on to the rocket with writing icing. Add decoration to the nose cone with piped lines and silver balls or dragées. Add the candles and candle-holders to the end of the Swiss rolls and light when ready to serve.

QUICK TIPS

★ If you are very short of time, simply place the rocket on a plain silver cake board or cover the cake board with grey marbled paper to achieve the same spacey results.

★ If the ice cream cone seems wobbly when stuck with jam, then insert a wooden skewer through it and into the cake.

★ Some candles drip heavily when lit, so protect the table or tablecloth with a plate or piece of foil.

full steam ahead

Serves 8 children
Decoration time: 30 minutes

2 x 300 g (10 oz) bought chocolate marble cakes
28 x 5 cm (11 x 2 inch) thin silver cake board
4 tablespoons smooth apricot jam
500 g (1 lb) red ready-to-roll icing
icing sugar or cornflour, for dusting
half a standard 15 cm (6 inch) jam or chocolate Swiss roll
75 g (3 oz) yellow ready-to-roll icing
8 round jam-filled or iced ring biscuits
1 tube red writing icing
2 large red jelly sweets
2 large yellow jelly sweets
200 g (7 oz) coloured jelly beans
1 candle and candle-holder

1 Trim the tops of the cakes to level them, if necessary. Place one cake near the end of the cake board. Cut one-third off the remaining cake for the cab and use the remaining piece for the tender. Spread the top and sides of all the cakes with jam.

2 Reserve one-third of the red icing, wrapped in clingfilm. Knead the remainder and roll out just over half on a surface lightly dusted with icing sugar or cornflour. Use to cover the engine base, smooth the surface, then trim off the excess. Re-roll the trimmings and amalgamate with the remaining kneaded icing. Use to cover the cab sides and the Swiss roll boiler, leaving the ends of the Swiss roll uncovered. Place the cab and boiler in position, securing them with jam if necessary. If the cab seems a little wobbly, insert a wooden skewer or plastic straw through the cab into the base.

3 Cover the tender in the same way with the reserved red icing, folding the edges of the icing over the top edge of the cake. Place the tender on the cake board behind the engine.

► *Jelly beans have been used to fill the tender here, but candy-covered chocolate drops, jelly babies or chocolate buttons could be used instead.*

4 Roll out the yellow icing on a surface dusted with icing sugar or cornflour and use to cover the cab top, to add rectangular windows and to cover the end of the Swiss roll boiler.

5 Stick the biscuits to the sides of the engine with red writing icing. Add jelly sweet buffers and lights, sticking them in place with red writing icing and pipe a number on front of the boiler. Fill the tender with sweets and complete the engine with a candle and candle-holder.

QUICK TIP

★ If you are having lots of children to a party, add extra trucks of sweets, made in the same way as the tender, and arrange the cake on a long strip of cardboard or a thin piece of wood, covered with foil or paper. You could add a chocolate finger biscuit track and sugar crystals or demerara sugar for gravel.

construction site cake

Serves 10 children
Decoration time: 25 minutes

**4 x 275 g (9 oz) bought or home-made Madeira Cakes
(see page 20) or angel cakes**
25 cm (10 inch) thin square cake board
4 tablespoons smooth apricot jam
double quantity chocolate Butter Icing (see page 23)
150 g (5 oz) white ready-to-roll icing
black paste food colouring
icing sugar or cornflour, for dusting
50 g (2 oz) dark chocolate
**selection small, plastic tip-up truck, diggers, lorries,
cement mixers, cars, stop signs and people**
candles and candle-holders (optional)

1 Place the cakes side by side on the cake board, sticking them together with jam, so that the narrowest ends of the cakes are towards you. Cut a triangle off the corner of two of the cakes, beginning at the centre of the cake furthest to the right and cutting down towards the corner of the second cake.

2 Cut this triangle in half through the middle. Butt one of the triangles against the diagonal cut and place the other triangle on the top left of the cake so that the cakes now form three levels. Trim the hard edges of the cake to make it look more like a sloping, tiered hill.

3 Spread butter icing over the top and sides of the cake, spreading a thin layer on the cake board too.

4 Reserve a little of the white ready-to-roll icing and wrap in clingfilm. Colour the remainder grey with a little black colouring. Roll out to a long thin strip about 40 x 5 cm (16 x 2 inches) on a surface lightly dusted with icing sugar or cornflour, trimming the sides if necessary. Drape the strip in a curve over the cake and make a break in the middle to suggest that the road is being repaired. Tear some of the icing trimmings into pieces and put into a tip-up truck for boulders.

5 Roll out the reserved white icing, cut it into thin strips and stick them on to the road with a little water. Grate some of the chocolate and chop the remainder, arrange it in piles on the cake with the diggers and other construction equipment. Add candles and candle-holders, if you like.

QUICK TIPS

★ If you would rather make your own cake, you will need a deep 28 x 18 cm (11 x 7 inch) chocolate or Victoria Sandwich Cake (see page 18) or Madeira Cake (see page 20).

★ Save some time and effort by mixing butter icing in a food processor, but make sure you dissolve the cocoa in boiling water first so that it doesn't taste raw.

◄ *Specialist cake-decorating shops stock a wide range of packs of coloured ready-to-roll icing, from pastel shades to vibrant primary colours, plus brown and black.*

flower garden

Serves 12 children
Decoration time: 30 minutes

12 bought or home-made Fairy Cakes (see page 19)
single quantity green Butter Icing (see page 23)
375 g (12 oz) white ready-to-roll icing
icing sugar or cornflour, for dusting
1 tube pink gel writing icing

1 Trim the tops of the cakes to level them, if necessary, then spread them with green butter icing.

2 Knead and roll out the white icing on a surface lightly dusted with icing sugar or cornflour. Stamp out flower shapes using 2.5 cm (1 inch) and 1 cm (½ inch) cutters. Curve the flowers by pressing into a clean, dry sponge or the cupped palm of your hand with the handle of a wooden spoon. Alternatively, if you have them, use plunger cutters.

3 Arrange the flowers randomly over the cakes. Finish each flower with a dot of pink gel icing. Arrange the cakes on a plate or cake board to serve.

QUICK TIPS

★ You can buy tiny cutters, often described as aspic cutters, in good cookshops, or specialist cake-decorating shops, where they may be available with easy-to-press-out plungers.

★ If you have lots of food to prepare for a party, cook the cakes in advance and pack into a plastic bag or box when cold. Prepare the butter icing in advance and put it in a small plastic box. Freeze both until the day before the party. Decorate the cakes the night before or on the morning of the party.

★ Adapt this idea for any design of tiny cutters that you have – try different-coloured numbers or tiny animals.

► *Use the same idea, but cover the fairy cakes with red butter icing and decorate with different sizes of red, pink and white heart shapes pressed on top. A great surprise for your loved ones.*

mermaid

Serves 6 children
Decoration time: 30 minutes

2 x 275 g (9 oz) bought striped angel cakes or
   plain Madeira Cakes (see page 20)
35 cm (14 inch) oval plain or iced cake board
double quantity pink Butter Icing (see page 23)
375 g (12 oz) turquoise, green or blue ready-to-roll icing
icing sugar or cornflour, for dusting
125 g (4 oz) pink ready-to-roll icing
1 tube each of yellow, black and red writing icing

1 Lay one of the cakes on its side on a chopping board. Cut it in half crossways, then shape one piece into an oval for the head. To make the other half into the body, cut triangular slices off the base for the waist and round the top corners for shoulders. Place these in position on the cake board.

2 Lay the second cake on its side and cut off the right-hand corner. Position the large piece at an angle to the body to make a tail, then arrange the trimmings at the end of the tail to curve slightly.

3 Spread the top and sides of the mermaid, including all the tail pieces, with butter icing. Knead the turquoise icing. Shape a piece into a 'Y', pinch the ends to a point and position at the end of the tail pieces. Roll out the remaining turquoise icing on a surface lightly dusted with icing sugar or cornflour and stamp out circles with a 2.5 cm (1 inch) round cutter. Starting at the base and working upwards, arrange the circles in an overlapping pattern over the tail.

4 To make the bikini, cut straps from the trimmings and complete with two circles. Roll a tiny ball of pink icing for the nose and position on to the face. Cut the remaining pink icing in half and shape into two arms. Stick them on to the side of the cake.

5 Pipe yellow hair with writing icing and add two black eyes and a red mouth.

▲ *By making just a few simple cuts, two basic cakes can be transformed into the curved body and tail of a mermaid.*

QUICK TIPS

★ If you don't have a cutter small enough for the scales, use the upturned end of a large piping tube, dusted with icing sugar or cornflour to the prevent the icing from sticking.

★ Change the colour of the hair to match the birthday girl.

★ To make marbled icing, knead in a little blue paste food colouring, but stop before it is completely mixed in.

★ If you can't find ready-coloured icing, make turquoise with blueberry and mint green paste food colouring.

★ Decorate the cake board with well-scrubbed seashells and pebbles, if you like.

best friends' tea party

Serves 4–5 children
Decoration time: 15 minutes

4 teaspoons smooth apricot jam
20 cm (8 inch) thin oval cake board
15 cm (6 inch) bought or home-made Victoria Sandwich
   Cake (see page 18)
200 g (7 oz) pale yellow ready-to-roll icing
icing sugar or cornflour, for dusting
250 g (8 oz) pink ready-to-roll icing
1 small white-iced round biscuit or marshmallow
1 candle and candle-holder
1 tube yellow writing icing
3 bendy plastic dolls about 15 cm (6 inches) tall
doll's house chairs, tea set and other accessories

1 Spread a little of the jam around the edge of the cake board and spread the remainder over the top of the cake.

2 Knead the yellow icing and roll out on a surface dusted with icing sugar or cornflour until slightly larger than the cake board. Lift on to the board and smooth with your fingertips. Trim off and reserve the excess. Mark the edge of the icing with a small, heart-shaped plunger cutter.

3 Knead and roll out the pink icing, then cut into a 23 cm (9 inch) circle, using a dinner plate as a guide. Cut out tiny heart shapes around the edge with the plunger cutter and reserve a few. Roll out the yellow icing trimmings to the same thickness as the pink icing. Stamp out hearts and press into the holes in the pink icing, then roll gently. Using a palette knife, lift and drape the tablecloth over the cake, smoothing the edges into folds with your fingertips.

4 Use some of the yellow trimmings to make a plate. Place the biscuit or marshmallow on it and top with the candle-holder and candle. Decorate the biscuit or marshmallow 'cake' with dots and garlands of yellow writing icing.

5 Bend the dolls to sit on the doll's house chairs and arrange them around the table. Place the cake on the table and add the tea set and any other accessories. Place the reserved pink hearts on the plates for napkins.

▲ *Add decoration to the icing tablecloth by stamping out small heart shapes and replacing them with the same size heart shapes cut from differently coloured icing.*

QUICK TIPS

★ If you are short of time, omit the heart-shaped decorations and stick some sugar flowers on to the edge of the tablecloth with a little writing icing.

★ If you don't have a cake-decorating shop nearby, use a 500 g (1 lb) pack of white ready-to-roll icing and colour it yourself.

MAD HATTER'S TEA PARTY
For Alice in Wonderland fans, make a long table out of a slice of Madeira cake and add some Different figures and assorted doll's house chairs to decorate.

ballet shoes

Serves 8–10 children
Decoration time: 25 minutes

2 x 23 cm (9 inch) bought chocolate Swiss rolls
3 tablespoons smooth apricot jam
500 g (1 lb) pink ready-to-roll icing
icing sugar or cornflour, for dusting
75 g (3 oz) white ready-to-roll icing
pink piping icing or jam
1.5 metres (1½ yards) pink satin ribbon

1 Using a serrated knife, trim the ends of the Swiss rolls into a curve. Scoop an oval out of the top of each cake, about 14 x 5 cm (5½ x 2 inches) and 2 cm (¾ inch) deep. Brush away any loose crumbs. Spread the cakes with jam.

2 Roll out half the pink icing on a surface dusted with icing sugar or cornflour. It should be at least 5 cm (2 inches) larger than the cake all the way around. Lift the icing over the rolling pin and drape it over a cake. Ease it over the sides, then smooth with your fingertips dusted with cornflour. Trim off the excess and wrap the trimmings in clingfilm. Transfer the iced cake to a baking sheet lined with nonstick baking paper.

3 Cover the second cake in the same way with the remaining pink icing and transfer to the baking sheet. Knead 25 g (1 oz) of the pink icing trimmings with the white icing, then cut it in half. Roll out one half to a 15 x 6 cm (6 x 2½ inch) oval. Press the oval into one ballet shoe and trim off the excess. Repeat with the remaining icing and the other shoe. Cut thin strips from the trimmings and shape into bows. Transfer the bows to the baking sheet to dry.

▲ *If you cannot find pink ready-to-roll icing you can adapt white icing to suit your needs. Just add red food colouring, a little at a time, until it has reached the desired shade.*

4 Shape the remaining pink icing into a long rope, then flatten with a rolling pin to 30 cm (12 inches) long. Cut the strip in half lengthways, then trim the outer edges with a fluted pastry wheel. Brush the top edges of the ballet shoes with water and press the strips around the join where the pale and darker pink icing meet. Add the icing bows, sticking them in place with a little piping icing or jam.

5 Leave the cakes to dry, if you have time, then arrange in a decorative box lined with patterned tissue paper or on an oval cake board covered with a thin layer of white ready-to-roll icing. Decorate with pink satin ribbons.

QUICK TIPS

★ Icing trimmings can be rolled out and cut into edible ribbons if you like.

★ If you are short of time, place the covered cakes straight on to a cake board and decorate immediately.

FOOTBALL CRAZY
To make football boots, shape the cake rolls as described above, but cover with black ready-to-roll icing with a paler grey liner. Add studs made with balls of black icing, coloured flashes made with strips of green or red ready-to-roll icing, and liquorice or black icing laces.

make a splash

Serves 8 children
Decoration time: 25 minutes

**18 cm (7 inch) bought or home-made Victoria
  Sandwich Cake (see page 19)**
double quantity blue Butter Icing (see page 23)
25 cm (10 inch) thin square silver cake board
250 g (8 oz) white ready-to-roll icing
icing sugar or cornflour, for dusting
250 g (8 oz) blue ready-to-roll icing
red paste food colouring
2 dolls, about 10 cm (4 inches) high
1 sugar flower
edible silver, gold and blue balls
small plastic boats
candles and candle-holders

1 Sandwich the cake layers together with a little butter icing and place on the cake board. Thinly spread the side of the cake with butter icing and then spread it more thickly over the top, roughing up the surface slightly to resemble water. Reserve the remaining butter icing.

2 Knead the white icing, cut in half and roll each piece into a long rope on a surface lightly dusted with icing sugar or cornflour. Trim the ropes to 60 cm (24 inches). Roll two blue ready-to-roll icing ropes in the same way.

3 Working quickly, arrange alternate coloured ropes up the side of the cake, beginning with a white rope and ending with a blue one. Trim the ends of the icing and press against the cake so that the ropes stick into the butter icing and jut slightly above the top of the cake.

4 Roll out some of the white icing trimmings and cut out a swimsuit. Press it on to one of the dolls and add thin ropes of icing for straps. Colour the remaining white icing red and dress the second doll in the same way. Shape the remaining red icing into a rectangular towel with a fringed edge. Make a blue rubber ring and place it on the cake board. Add the towel, candles and candle-holders and dots of the remaining blue butter icing to represent puddles.

▲ *To make the side of the pool, arrange alternate blue and white ropes up the side of the cake, pressing them into the butter icing.*

5 Complete the red swimsuit with the sugar flower and the white one with coloured balls, sticking them in place with a little butter icing. Add plastic boats to the pool.

QUICK TIP

★ For children who don't like butter icing, use jam to sandwich the cake layers together and to cover the sides. Make a lemon jelly, according to the packet instructions, adding a little green food colouring to turn it blue. Allow the jelly to set in a shallow dish, then chop it up and arrange on the top of the cake for water.

it's my birthday

Serves 6 children
Decoration time: 30 minutes

**18 cm (7 inch) bought or home-made Victoria
  Sandwich Cake (see page 19)**
20 cm (8 inch) thin square cake board
double quantity pink Butter Icing (see page 23)
4 tablespoons strawberry jam
500 g (1 lb) white ready-to-roll icing
icing sugar or cornflour, for dusting
1 tube white piping icing
2 x 6 cm (2½ inch) thick, non-drip white or pink candles
20 g (¾ oz) pack of sugar flowers

❚ *Cut out a paper circle the same size as the cake and fold
it into a wedge shape to use as a guide for cutting the cake
layers. Piece the trimmings together to make a third layer,
cutting off any surplus and filling in the centre with offcuts.*

1 Using the cake tin as a guide, cut a circle of paper the same
size as the Victoria sandwich cake layers. Fold it into a wedge
shape, retaining the curved edge. Using the folded paper as a
guide, cut the cake layers into wedge shapes. Piece the
trimmings together on the folded paper, trimming again where
necessary, to make a third wedge.

2 Place one wedge on the cake board, and spread thickly with
butter icing so that the icing protrudes slightly over the edge. Dot
with half the jam, again adding some near the edges of the cake.
Cover with the separate pieces of cake and spread with butter
icing and jam as before, then top with the third wedge.

3 Spread the top and rounded side of the cake with a very thin
layer of butter icing. Knead the white ready-to-roll icing and roll
out on a surface lightly dusted with icing sugar or cornflour to
make a 28 x 25 cm (11 x 10 inch triangle). Drape the icing over
the cake and smooth into place with your fingertips dusted with
a little icing sugar or cornflour.

4 Trim the icing to the exact shape of the cake. Brush any
crumbs off the trimmings, knead again and re-roll. Cut moon
shapes about 10 cm (4 inches) long to make swags. Curl the long
edges up, then drape around the side of the cake and secure
with white piping icing.

5 Pipe rosettes of pink butter icing between the swags and
around the top and bottom edges of the cake with a large star
tube. Decorate the cake with the sugar flowers. Pipe larger
rosettes on top of the cake and press a candle into the
centre of each.

QUICK TIPS

★ Cover the cake and board with a plastic cake dome or a large
  upturned bowl so that the cut edges do not dry out. Do not
  use clingfilm or foil in case you damage the soft butter icing.

★ For a more contemporary look, use different-coloured icing
  and replace the flowers with jelly diamonds or other sweets.

doll's house

Serves 20 children
Decoration time: 30 minutes

5 x 350 g (11½ oz) bought chocolate marble loaf cakes
quadruple quantity pink Butter Icing (see page 23)
30 cm (12 inch) thin round cake board, plain or iced
9 pale pink rectangular iced biscuits
100 g (3½ oz) midget gems or other small fruit gums
200 g (7 oz) jelly beans
9 pale yellow rectangular iced biscuits
4 pieces pale green fruit rock
1 tube yellow writing icing
selection of icing flowers
few white chocolate buttons

1 Trim the tops and a little off the sides of four of the cakes so that they stack together closely to make a house, two cakes wide and two cakes high. Sandwich the cakes together with butter icing on the cake board, then spread a little on the top. Cut the last cake in half diagonally and butt the halves together to make the roof.

2 Cover the sides and roof of the house thickly with butter icing. Arrange the pink biscuits overlapping to make the roof tiles. Arrange the midget gems or fruit gums along the ridge of the roof. Stick the jelly beans under the eaves, down the edges of the house and around the bottom.

3 Stick two yellow biscuits to each side of the house to make windows and another for a door at one end. Cut the rock in half with a serrated knife and press on to the cake under the windows. Pipe on window bars with yellow icing, then pipe on dots of icing and stick the flowers in place. Attach a midget gem or fruit gum door knob.

4 Add a few extra flowers to the cake board and use white chocolate buttons to make a path to the front door.

▲ *Butt four loaf cakes together, two cakes high and two cakes wide, to make the main shape of the house, and then cut the fifth cake in half diagonally and but together to make the roof.*

QUICK TIPS

★ You can cover the cake board with 250 g (8 oz) ready-to-roll pale green coloured icing. Stick the edges with a little apricot jam. Trim the edges of the icing and leave to harden before placing the cake on top.

★ Vary the types of sweets and biscuits. You could also try an all-chocolate version with White Chocolate Fudge Frosting (see page 24) or vanilla Butter Icing (see page 23) with chocolate-covered biscuits and sweets for decorations.

★ If you are making the cake the day before the party, don't add the biscuits to the roof until the last minute as the moisture from the butter icing will make them go soft.

★ For Christmas, the house could be covered with royal icing for snow, with piped icicles at the windows and under the eaves. Add a dusting of icing sugar to the biscuits on the roof.

little fishes

Serves 12 children
Decoration time: 25 minutes

200 g (7 oz) luxury white cooking chocolate
12 bought or home-made Fairy Cakes (see page 19)
12 fan wafer biscuits
2 x 75 g (3 oz) packs white chocolate buttons
100 g (3½ oz) tub sugar strands
12 mini candy-covered chocolate drops
1 tube red writing icing
edible coloured balls

1 Break the white chocolate into pieces and melt in a heatproof bowl set over a saucepan of just boiled water for 2–3 minutes.

2 Meanwhile, trim the tops of the cakes level, if necessary. Cut each fan biscuit in half, and cut one half in half again. Trim off the points of the biscuits and discard.

3 Stir the chocolate and spread a rounded teaspoonful over the top of each cake. Spread the large pieces of wafer biscuit thinly with the chocolate, then position on the cakes for tails. Spread the smaller pieces with the chocolate and press two on to each cake for fins.

4 Arrange overlapping white chocolate buttons on the fish bodies for scales. Put the cakes on a tray, then sprinkle sugar strands over the fins and tails. Stick a chocolate-drop eye on to each fish with a little melted chocolate and pipe on red mouths. Leave the chocolate to harden in a cool place.

5 When you are ready to serve, arrange the cakes on a cake board or plate with coloured balls to resemble bubbles.

► *Cut the fan wafers in half, then cut one of the pieces in half again and trim off the pointed ends to make the fish fins and tail.*

★ The cakes can be made in bulk and frozen in a plastic box until required. Simply take out as many as you need and decorate while still partly frozen or after about 30 minutes.

OTHER FISH TOO
Vary the colours and types of the fish by covering them with milk chocolate and white chocolate buttons, or by using white chocolate buttons coated with sugar strands. The tails and fins can also be sprinkled with grated white chocolate or milk chocolate strands, or left plain, if preferred.

in the jungle

Serves 12 children
Decoration time: 30 minutes

12 bought or home-made Fairy Cakes (see page 19)
icing sugar or cornflour, for dusting
4 tablespoons smooth apricot jam or vanilla Butter
Icing (see page 23), plus extra jam for fixing on
decorations
ELEPHANTS
250 g (8 oz) white ready-to-roll icing
black paste food colouring
1 tube black writing icing
PANDAS
175 g (6 oz) white ready-to-roll icing
black paste food colouring
1 tube black writing icing
TIGERS
175 g (6 oz) white ready-to-roll icing
brown, red and yellow paste food colourings
1 tube black writing icing
LIONS
175 g (6 oz) white ready-to-roll icing
brown and yellow paste food colourings
50 g (2 oz) dark chocolate, melted
6 brown candy-covered chocolate drops
FROGS
250 g (8 oz) white ready-to-roll icing
green paste food colouring
12 yellow candy-covered chocolate drops
1 tube red writing icing

1 Trim the tops of the cakes level, if necessary, then spread with jam or butter icing.

2 ELEPHANTS To make the elephants, reserve a small ball of white icing for the tusks and wrap in clingfilm. Colour the remainder grey with a little black colouring. Wrap and reserve half of the icing and roll out the rest on a surface lightly dusted with icing sugar or cornflour. Stamp out 6 x 6 cm (2½ inch) rounds with a fluted biscuit cutter and press on to the cakes, re-rolling the icing if necessary. Shape small balls of grey icing into trunks, make a hole in the end with a cocktail stick and stick on to the cakes with a little jam. Roll out the reserved grey icing

and cut ear shapes with a small knife. Stick on to the cakes with jam and add moulded white tusks and small piped black eyes.

3 PANDAS To make the pandas, colour one-third of the icing black and wrap tightly in clingfilm. Roll out the remainder, stamp out 6 x 6 cm (2½ inch) fluted rounds and press on to the cakes. Shape tiny balls of black icing, flatten them between your finger and thumb and cut in half for ears. Make black muzzles in the same way with slightly larger circles and stick them on to the cakes with jam. Add tiny white eyes and black noses from the trimmings. Pipe on black pupils and mouths.

4 TIGERS To make the tigers, reserve a tiny ball of white icing and wrap in clingfilm. Colour a walnut-size ball of icing brown and wrap. Colour the remainder orange with red and yellow colouring, then roll out on a surface dusted with icing sugar or cornflour. Cut 6 x 6 cm (2½ inch) rounds with a fluted biscuit cutter and press on to the cakes. Use the trimmings to make ears with brown triangles and stick on to the cakes with jam. Roll out the remaining brown icing, cut thin strips and stick on to the cakes with water. Shape the trimmings into small balls for noses. Add tiny balls of white icing for eyes and press on to the cakes. Pipe on black pupils and mouths.

5 LIONS To make the lions, reserve a tiny ball of white icing for the eyes and wrap in clingfilm. Colour a walnut-sized ball of icing brown and wrap. Colour the remainder yellow, roll out on a surface dusted lightly with icing sugar or cornflour and cut 6 x 6 cm (2½ inch) fluted rounds with a biscuit cutter, then press them on to the cakes. Add yellow whiskers. Shape tiny white balls for the eyes and press them on to the cakes. Shape small rounds of brown for the ears. Spoon the melted chocolate into a greaseproof paper piping bag and snip off the tip. Pipe squiggles

of chocolate around the edge of the lions' faces for manes, add dots to the eyes, pipe on mouths and stick on brown chocolate-drop noses and the icing ears.

6 FROGS To make the frogs, colour all the icing green. Roll out half on a surface dusted with icing sugar or cornflour. Cut 6 x 6 cm (2½ inch) fluted rounds with a biscuit cutter and press them on to the cakes. Shape small balls for the eyes, flatten between your fingers and stick them on to the cakes with jam, adding yellow candy-covered chocolate-drop eyeballs. Shape thin ropes of icing for mouths, fold in half, pinch the ends and press them on to the cakes. Make ropes of icing for the legs about 10 cm (4 inches) long, pinch into a 'Z' shape, then flatten with your fingertips to look like legs. Mark webbed feet with a small knife and stick them on to the cakes with jam. Pipe on red pupils.

QUICK TIP

★ Keep a supply of cup cakes in the freezer. They defrost at room temperature in around an hour and can be decorated while still frozen.

my first piggy bank

Serves 10 children
Decoration time: 25 minutes

**18 cm (7 inch) bought or home-made Victoria
  Sandwich Cake (see page 19)**
**2 bought or home-made Fairy Cakes (see page 19) or
  American Muffins (see page 21)**
double quantity Butter Icing (see page 23)
red paste food colouring
20 cm (8 inch) oval silver cake board
125 g (4 oz) white ready-to-roll icing
icing sugar or cornflour, for dusting
2 candy-covered chocolate drops
1 tube black writing icing
2 packs foil-covered chocolate coins

1 Put the cake layers one on top of the other on a chopping
board and trim a little off the top and bottom to make an oval pig
shape. Trim the cake on one side to make the head and snout.
Trim the tops of the little cakes to level, if necessary.

2 Colour the butter icing pink, then spread it over the top and
sides of the little cakes. Place them, slightly spaced apart, on the
cake board. Sandwich together the cake layers with butter icing
and then spread a thin layer of the icing all over the top and
sides to stick the crumbs in place. Add a second thicker layer of
icing. Carefully stand the sponge cake on the legs and spread
icing over the other side. Prop up the cake with a couple of large
cans to prevent it from toppling over.

3 Shape two small ovals from the white ready-to-roll icing for
eyes and stick them on to the cake. Colour the remaining ready-
to-roll icing pink with a little red colouring, then, with your
fingers dusted with icing sugar or cornflour, shape two ears, a
curly tail, strips to mark the money slot and a small round nose.
Mark nostrils in the nose with the end of a teaspoon, then press
all of these on to the cake.

4 Stick the candy-covered chocolate drops on to the eyes with
a little black piping icing, then pipe on black eyelashes. Scatter
foil-covered coins around the board and press one into the top
of the cake. Leave until ready to serve.

★ If you want to re-use an old cake board, but it looks a bit tatty,
  spread it thinly with a little apricot jam and cover with a thin
  layer of white or coloured ready-to-roll icing.

★ If you haven't got time to make butter icing, cover the cake
  with pale pink ready-to-roll icing.

★ If you are not having your child's party at home, lay the cake
  flat on a 28 cm (11 inch) round cake board so that it is easy to
  transport.

▼ *Cut a plain round Victoria sandwich cake into an oval
shape, then trim away one side to make a snout and add
fairy cakes for legs.*

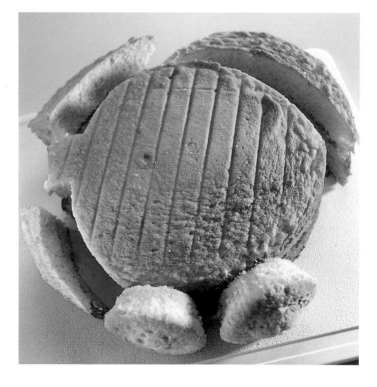

space bugs

Serves 12 children
Decoration time: 25 minutes

**12 chocolate or plain, bought or home-made Fairy Cakes
   (see page 19)**
4 tablespoons chocolate spread
375 g (12 oz) red ready-to-roll icing
icing sugar or cornflour, for dusting
12 chocolate-covered marshmallows
12 chocolate sticks
1 tube red writing icing
1 pack mini candy-covered chocolate drops
1 tube black writing icing

❗ *Roll out the red icing, stamp out a round the same size as the top of the cake, then cut a small semi-circle and halve the remaining icing to make the wings.*

1 Leave the cakes in their paper cases and trim the tops to level them, if necessary. Spread the cakes with chocolate spread.

2 Knead the red ready-to-roll icing on a surface lightly dusted with icing sugar or cornflour, then roll out and cut 12 x 5.5 cm (2¼ inch) rounds using a plain biscuit cutter. Cut a little off the top of each round using the same cutter, then cut the remaining shapes in half to make wings. Press the wings on to the cakes so that the tips are slightly apart. Re-roll the trimmings as needed and continue until all the cakes are covered.

3 Add the marshmallows for heads, sticking them in place with a little extra chocolate spread, if necessary. Halve the chocolate sticks and press two behind the heads for antennae. Pipe on red smiling mouths, then pipe dots of red icing over the wings and stick on the sweets. Add chocolate-drop eyes to the faces and the tops of the antennae in the same way. Using black icing, pipe dots on the eyes. Arrange the bugs on a cake board or plate. Leave in a cool place to harden.

QUICK TIPS

✱ If you don't have a biscuit cutter the right size, then use an upturned glass as a template.

✱ Look out for ready-coloured icing from specialist cake-decorating shops. While supermarkets do sell coloured icing, it is usually in a box containing three or four small packs of different colours and can be expensive if you only need one. Alternatively, buy white icing and colour it yourself with red paste colouring.

FOR HALLOWEEN
Make up death-watch or dung beetles with brown or black ready-to-roll icing. Omit the spots or pipe on squiggly markings with tubes of coloured writing icing.

busy bees

Serves 12 children
Decoration time: 20 minutes

12 bought or home-made Fairy Cakes (see page 19)
double quantity Butter Icing (see page 23)
2 teaspoons cocoa powder dissolved in 2 teaspoons
boiling water
yellow paste food colouring
2 teaspoons milk
3 sheets edible rice paper
24 dolly-mixture sweets
1 tube red writing icing
24 edible silver balls

1 Leaving the paper cases on the cakes, trim the tops of the cakes to level them, if necessary. Divide the butter icing between two bowls and stir the cocoa paste into one batch and yellow colouring and the milk into the other.

2 Spoon the yellow butter icing into a greaseproof paper piping bag and snip off the tip. Pipe lines over the cakes, leaving a gap the same width as the piped icing between them. Spoon chocolate icing into a second piping bag and repeat, filling in the gaps between the yellow icing strips.

3 Cut each sheet of rice paper into four. Fold the pieces and cut wing shapes, but do not cut through the fold. Open out and arrange the wings on the cakes. Add dolly-mixture eyes, pipe on small dots of red and add silver balls. Pipe on small red mouths and arrange on a cake board or plate to serve.

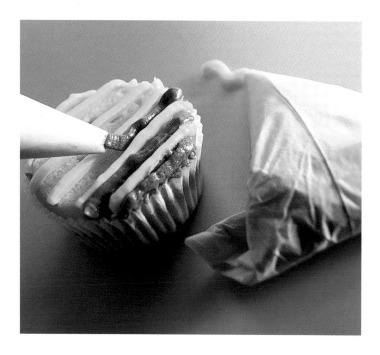

▴ *Pipe lines of yellow butter icing over the cakes, leaving a small space between, then fill in the spaces with piped lines of chocolate butter icing.*

QUICK TIPS

✱ Dissolving the cocoa in boiling water gives it a mellow taste. If the chocolate icing is very soft, chill in the refrigerator for 15 minutes before piping.

✱ Black paste colouring could be used instead of cocoa powder, if preferred.

✱ If the weather is very hot, chill the cakes in the refrigerator.

✱ Get the children to make their own paper plates with heavy cardboard cut into the shape of large sunflowers or roses, or cut plates from old cereal packets and paint flowers on top.

BEAUTIFUL BUTTERFLIES
Spread half the cakes with chocolate icing and the other half with yellow or pink icing. Cut wing shapes as for the bees, but then ask the children to draw on designs using pens with edible ink, available from cookshops and specialist cake-decorating shops.

millie the millipede

Serves 10 children
Decoration time: 20 minutes

9 home-made mini Cup Cakes (see page 18)
1 home-made standard Fairy Cake (see page 19)
2 tablespoons smooth apricot jam
30 x 12 cm (12 x 5 inch) thin green cake board
125 g (4 oz) red ready-to-roll icing
icing sugar or cornflour, for dusting
125 g (4 oz) green ready-to-roll icing
2 yellow candy-covered chocolate drops

1 Trim the tops of the cakes to level them, if necessary, leaving the paper cases on. Spread the cakes with jam and arrange them on the cake board to look like a curved millipede with the large cake for the head.

2 Lightly knead the red icing, then roll out on a surface lightly dusted with icing sugar or cornflour. Cut a head using a 6 cm (2½ inch) fluted biscuit cutter and press on top of the larger cake. Cut the remaining red icing into 1.5 cm (¾ inch) squares and then cut a triangle out of one side to make legs. Stick two legs on to each cake. Cut a large triangle for the tail and place on the end cake.

3 Knead the green icing and roll out. Cut out a 5.5 cm (2¼ inch) round using a plain biscuit cutter and place it on the larger cake. Stamp out smaller rounds using a 3 cm (1¼ inch) plain round biscuit cutter or upturned piping nozzle. Using the edge of the cutter, cut a little curved section away from one side, then repeat on the other side. Position these shapes on the little cakes for the millipede body.

4 Re-roll any green trimmings and add two rounds to the head for eyes and finish with yellow chocolate drops stuck in place with jam. Roll a thin rope and position for the mouth. Leave in a cool place until ready to serve.

► *Stamp out green icing rounds to make the millipede head and body, then shape the body pieces by cutting away semi-circles, using the edge of a round cutter. Make sure that the legs are visible.*

SAMANTHA THE SNAKE
To make a snake, omit the legs and vary the colour scheme to match a child's favourite snake. Pipe on markings with tubes of writing icing.

QUICK TIPS

★ Vary the colour of the millipede depending on what coloured icing you can obtain.

★ Millipede legs can also be made with chocolate sticks, broken into pieces.

★ Your child's name could be piped along the body of the millipede, adding a letter to the top of each little cake.

the doyouthinkhesawus dinosaur

Serves 10 children
Decoration time: 30 minutes

**23 cm (9 inch) round home-made Madeira Cake
(see page 20)**
6 tablespoons smooth apricot jam
25 x 35 cm (10 x 14 inch) thin rectangular cake board
500 g (1 lb) white ready-to-roll icing
green, blue and yellow paste food colourings
icing sugar or cornflour, for dusting
250 g (8 oz) red ready-to-roll icing
50 g (2 oz) pack candy-covered chocolate drops
1 tube yellow writing icing
few sugar crystals

1 Cut a 4 cm (1½ inch) strip from the centre of the cake, then sandwich together the half-moon shapes with some of the jam. Stand the cake on the board so that the curved sides are uppermost. Halve the remaining strip of cake and use one half for the head, rounding off the corners to make the snout and back of the head. Use the other half for the tail, cutting a diagonal slice off the length of the tail piece. Turn it around and butt the pieces together to lengthen the tail. Brush the top and sides of the cake with jam.

2 Knead the white icing to soften it, then knead in a little green colouring until evenly coloured. Add more green, blue and yellow colourings and knead briefly for a marbled effect. Roll out on a surface lightly dusted with icing sugar or cornflour until large enough to cover the dinosaur. Drape the icing over the cake, smooth the surface and trim off the excess. Cut a triangle for the end of the tail, shape legs, eyes and nostrils from the trimmings and stick them on to the cake with the remaining jam.

3 Knead the red icing. Shape small balls of the icing into triangles and press them along the top of the dinosaur for back spines. Roll out and cut a tongue, then press on to the mouth.

4 Stick the sweets on to the dinosaur's back and eye sockets with yellow writing icing, then pipe on eyeballs. Sprinkle sugar crystals on to the board around the dinosaur.

◄ *Knead a little green paste colouring into white ready-to-roll icing until evenly coloured, then streak with more green, plus blue and yellow colourings. Knead until only partially blended, then roll out for an eye-catching marbled effect.*

★ The cake could be flavoured with a little grated orange rind and then sandwiched together with one quantity of plain or orange-flavoured Butter Icing (see page 23).

★ Recycle old cake boards and cover marks or scratches with new foil or coloured ready-to-roll icing, sticking it in place with a little jam, or desiccated coconut.

★ A 38 cm (15 inch) oval cake board could also be used.

chocolate hedgehogs

Serves 6 children
Decoration time: 20 minutes

6 bought or home-made Fairy Cakes (see page 19)
single quantity Dark Chocolate Fudge Frosting
(see page 25)
3 flaked chocolate bars, cut into thin pieces
3 glacé cherries, halved
12 edible silver balls or mini candy-covered
chocolate drops
125 g (4 oz) red ready-to-roll icing
icing sugar or cornflour, for dusting

1 Remove cake cases and cut a triangular snout in each cake. Place them on a wire rack set over a large plate.

2 Spoon warm chocolate frosting over the cakes until they are completely covered. Working quickly, stick pieces of flaked chocolate over two-thirds of each cake for hedgehog spines. Add cherry noses and silver-ball or chocolate-drop eyes.

3 Carefully lift the hedgehogs on to a cake board or plate, trimming away any surplus icing around the base.

FOR PINK MICE
Coat cakes in a thick pale pink glacé icing, butter icing or ready-to-roll icing. Shape small balls of ready-to-roll icing into ear shapes and add long curled ropes of icing for tails. Shape pale pink whiskers or use snipped pieces of strawberry bootlace sweets. Add cherry noses and silver-ball eyes as above.

★ If children are helping you to make these cakes, it may be easier to ice and decorate them one at a time, as the icing sets quickly. This makes it more difficult to press the chocolate spines on to the cakes.

★ Nestle hedgehogs on a grassy board by colouring a little desiccated coconut with liquid green food colouring and spooning it around the finished cakes.

★ Peaked fairy cakes are best for this. If yours are quite flat, then use cakes in pairs, sandwiched together with chocolate icing. Use petit-four size cakes for younger children.

► *Cut two slices off each fairy cake at angles, for a quick but effective triangular snout.*

aquarium

Serves 12 children
Decoration time: 30 minutes

**30 x 23 x 5cm (12 x 9 x 2 inch) home-made chocolate
    traybake Madeira Cake (see page 20)**
triple quantity blue Butter Icing (see page 23)
30 x 20 cm (12 x 8 inch) thin silver cake board
75 g (3 oz) each green, yellow and red ready-to-roll icing
icing sugar or cornflour, for dusting
3 black mini candy-covered chocolate drops
250 g (8 oz) black ready-to-roll icing
2 tablespoons brown sugar crystals

1 Halve the cake to make 2 x 23 x 15 cm (9 x 6 inch) rectangles,
then sandwich them together with butter icing. Spread the large
side with butter icing, then stand the cake on one of the long
thin sides on the cake board. Spread the other sides with the
remaining butter icing.

2 Knead the green ready-to-roll icing and roll out on a surface
lightly dusted with icing sugar or cornflour. Cut out weed shapes
with a small knife and press them on to the cake.

3 Knead a little yellow icing and shape into three small ropes
about 5 cm (2 inches) long. Make four small red ropes from half
the red icing in the same way. Butt up the red and yellow ropes
so that the colours alternate, then roll flat. Cut a fish shape,
make small cuts in the fins and tails and place on the cake. Roll
out half of the remaining red icing and cut a second fish shape.
Roll out a little yellow icing, then cut tiny rounds with the tip of a
5 mm (¼ inch) plain piping tube. Cut out rounds from the red fish
body and replace with yellow rounds. Flatten slightly with a
rolling pin and press the fish on to the cake.

4 Re-roll the red trimmings and cut out a seahorse. Place it on
the cake, lifting the green weed and sliding it underneath, if you
like. Add mini chocolate-drop eyes.

5 Knead and roll out the black icing. Cut 1.5 cm (¾ inch) wide
strips and press them on to the sides, top and base of the tank,
trimming the lengths as necessary. Press sugar on to the base of
the tank for gravel. Leave in a cool place until required.

▲ *To make stripy fish, butt ropes of yellow and red icing
together, roll out flat to stick the colours together, then cut
fish shapes with a small knife.*

QUICK TIPS

★ If you don't have time to make a cake, cut 4 slices of
bought Madeira cake and sandwich them together with
a little butter icing.

★ Butter icing can be spread quite roughly over the cake to
give a watery effect, since much of it is covered with fish and
pond weed.

★ If you are really short of time, then you could raid the toy box
or bathroom and use some plastic fish. Make sure they're
well washed.

★ If you need to transport the cake to a party venue, make the
fish tank flat on the cake board and use a slightly larger board,
23 x 18 cm (9 x 7 inches), instead.

easter chicks

Serves 8 children
Decoration time: 25 minutes

8 bought or home-made Fairy Cakes (see page 19)
double quantity citrus Butter Icing, coloured yellow
   (see page 23)
250 g (8 oz) yellow ready-to-roll icing
icing sugar or cornflour, for dusting
125 g (4 oz) orange ready-to-roll icing
16 edible silver balls

1 Remove the paper cases, spear each cake with a fork and spread the tops and sides thickly with butter icing.

2 Knead the yellow ready-to-roll icing on a surface lightly dusted with icing sugar or cornflour. Shape eight small balls from some of the icing and stick them to the cakes for chick heads. Dot the tops with a little butter icing.

3 Roll out the remaining yellow icing and stamp out eight 5 cm (2 inch) rounds with a plain biscuit cutter, re-rolling the trimmings as necessary. Cut the rounds in half and mark the edges with a small knife to resemble feathers. Press them on to the sides of the chicks.

4 Shape tiny triangles of orange icing and stick them on to the chick heads with a little water for beaks. Roll the remainder into thin ropes and cut into 16 x 5 cm (2 inch) lengths. Make two slits in the end of each piece for legs and feet and then stick the chick bodies on to the legs with any remaining butter icing. Arrange on a plate or cake board.

► *Get the children to help shape ball-like heads, easy-to-cut wings and simple rope-like legs for these fun chicks.*

QUICK TIPS

★ If you can't buy ready-coloured icing, then mix white ready-to-roll icing with a little red and yellow paste colourings to make orange.

★ Mascarpone Frosting (see page 25) could also be used to decorate the cakes.

★ Ready-made muffins could also be used, but, as they are a little larger, you will have only enough butter icing for the chicks. If you have tiny children, you could also make mini versions with cakes or muffins made in petit-four size cases.

★ You could also serve these cakes on a cake board, sprinkled with grated white chocolate and broken eggshells to suggest the chicks had just hatched. Alternatively, arrange them on a chocolate cake decorated with chocolate sticks placed around the top and sides to resemble a nest.

easter nests

Serves 8 children
Decoration time: 10 minutes

125 g (4 oz) luxury dark cooking chocolate
50 g (2 oz) butter
2 tablespoons golden syrup
75 g (3 oz) or 3 shredded wheat breakfast cereal
115 g (3¾ oz) pack mini chocolate eggs
8 mini yellow chicks

1 Break the chocolate into pieces and put them into a saucepan with the butter and golden syrup. Heat gently, stirring until the chocolate and butter have melted.

2 Tear the breakfast cereal into pieces and stir it into the chocolate mixture. Stir well to coat the cereal in the chocolate, then spoon the mixture into mounds on a baking sheet lined with nonstick baking paper. Leave to cool and harden.

3 Divide the eggs between the nests and chill until firm. Transfer the nests to a plate or 20 cm (8 inch) cake board. Add the chicks just before serving.

QUICK TIPS

★ Cornflakes or puffed rice breakfast cereal can be used instead of the wheat cereal for a change.

★ The chocolate, syrup and butter can be heated in the microwave for 2 minutes on full power. If children are doing this, warn them that, although the bowl won't be hot, the ingredients will, so they should handle them with care.

★ Speed up the setting time by chilling the nests in the refrigerator.

★ The chocolate mixture can be spooned into paper cake cases, if you prefer.

★ Make teeny tiny nests for very young children and add eggs shaped from pastel-coloured ready-to-roll icing, or use mini candy-covered chocolate drops.

► *Children of all ages love these cute little yellow chicks. Look for them in sweetshops and specialist cake-decorating shops.*

chocolate bunnies

Makes 8
Decoration time: 15 minutes

**30 x 23 cm (12 x 9 inch) home-made chocolate traybake
 Madeira Cake (see page 20)**
single quantity Chocolate Ganache (see page 25)
40 g (1½ oz) milk chocolate buttons
8 mini marshmallows
1 tube yellow writing icing
24 edible silver balls

1 Cut the cake into eight rabbit shapes by using a 12 cm (5 inch) rabbit biscuit cutter, topping and tailing the shapes so that the minimum amount of cake is wasted. Place the cakes on a wire rack set over a tray.

2 Carefully spoon warm chocolate ganache over the cakes and smooth it over them with a small palette knife, touching up any missed bits.

3 Add chocolate buttons for feet and mini marshmallows for tails. Pipe on yellow whiskers and add silver balls for eyes and a nose. Leave to set, then transfer to a serving plate or cake board.

QUICK TIPS

★ If you want to get ahead, plain rabbit cakes can be frozen, then iced while still partly frozen for a quick-setting icing.

★ Melted white chocolate could also be used to pipe on features, once the ganache has set.

★ If you are having trouble smoothing the icing, dip the palette knife into boiling water. The warmth of the knife will soon make any lines disappear.

▲ *Top and tail the rabbit cutter so that only the minimum amount of cake is wasted. If you don't have a cutter this shape or size, then improvise and draw a rabbit shape on to cardboard – an empty cereal packet is ideal. Cut it out with scissors and use it as a template, cutting around the shape with a small pointed knife.*

three naughty kittens

Serves 4 children
Decoration time: 30 minutes

8 bought or home-made Fairy Cakes (see page 19)
single quantity red Butter Icing (see page 23)
200 g (7 oz) strawberry-flavoured bootlaces
20 cm (8 inch) thin round silver cake board
250 g (8 oz) black ready-to-roll icing
icing sugar or cornflour, for dusting
75 g (3 oz) white ready-to-roll icing
1 tube black writing icing

1 Trim the tops of the cakes to level them, if necessary. Spread a little butter icing over the cake tops and sandwich them together in pairs. Spread butter icing thinly all over the tops and sides of the cakes.

2 Wrap the strawberry bootlaces around the cakes to resemble balls of wool, reserving a few spare strands. Arrange the 'balls of wool' on the cake board and twist the remaining bootlaces between them.

3 To make the kittens, mould a 3.5 cm (1½ inch) long oval of black icing with your fingers dusted with icing sugar or cornflour. Position it on top of, or at the base of, a cake and add a small head about 1.5 cm (¾ inch) in diameter. Shape four small legs and a tail and press them on to the body. Make ears with tiny balls of white icing wrapped in black and press them on to the kitten. Add tiny ropes of white for whiskers and stick on with dots of black writing icing. Add tiny balls of white for paws.

4 Repeat to make a second seated black cat in the same way, but add a circle of white icing to the tummy. Knead the remaining black and white icing together, shape into a tabby cat and arrange on a ball of wool.

► *Wrap strawberry bootlace sweets around the cakes so that the butter icing is completely covered.*

★ Three kittens have been added to the cakes, but you may prefer to make an extra one so that each child has one of his or her own to keep or eat.

★ If you are very short of time, buy little plastic cats from a toy or cake-decorating shop.

★ One large ball of wool could be made with two cakes made the old-fashioned way in pudding basins, and two larger cats.

★ For very little children, cut the cakes in half to serve.

wicked witches

Makes 4
Decoration time: 20 minutes

4 ice cream cones
75 g (3 oz) dark or milk luxury cooking chocolate, melted
4 chocolate-covered or plain digestive biscuits
single quantity green Butter Icing (see page 23)
4 bought or home-made chocolate-chip American Muffins
    (see page 21)
50 g (2 oz) red strawberry-flavoured bootlaces
4 different-coloured dolly-mixture sweets
4 different-coloured jelly sweets
1 tube black writing icing
32 x 12 cm (13 x 5 inch) green cake board

1 Trim the curved tops off the ice cream cones with a serrated knife and discard. Spread a little melted chocolate over each biscuit, then spread the remainder over the outside of the ice cream cones. Stick the cones on to the biscuits to make the witches' hats and leave for 5 minutes to set.

2 Spread butter icing all over the muffins. Cut the bootlaces into 12–15 cm (5–6 inch) lengths and press them on to the muffins for hair. Halve the dolly mixtures, attach them to the muffin faces for eyes. Stick on jelly sweet noses, then pipe on black eyebrows and jagged angry mouths.

3 Dot the remaining butter icing on top of the bootlace sweets and stick the hats in place. Arrange the witches on a cake board or plate to serve.

► *These funky strawberry- and apple-flavoured bootlaces are a great alternative to the more traditional liquorice bootlaces, which children sometimes do not like.*

QUICK TIPS

✱ Make these witches look even more sinister by serving on a black china plate, black paper-covered cake board or black marble cheese board.

✱ Hats, hair and facial features can be added to scoops of vanilla or strawberry ice cream instead.

✱ To make more cakes, simply multiply the quantities to suit party numbers.

haunted house

Serves 15 children
Decoration time: 30 minutes

150 g (5 oz) luxury dark or milk cooking chocolate
1 jumbo 30 cm (12 inch) bought chocolate Swiss roll
1 standard 15 cm (6 inch) bought chocolate Swiss roll
23 cm (9 inch) thin round cake board
3 ice cream cones
200 g (7 oz) milk chocolate buttons
125 g (4 oz) white ready-to-roll icing
brown paste food colouring
icing sugar or cornflour, for dusting
2 teaspoons smooth apricot jam
1 tube black writing icing
Halloween candles and candle-holders

1 Break the chocolate into pieces and put it into a large, heatproof bowl set over a saucepan of just boiled water. Leave for 2–3 minutes, until just melted. Meanwhile, cut one-third off the large Swiss roll.

2 Spread a thin layer of melted chocolate over the cake board and stand all the Swiss roll pieces up on their ends, touching each other to resemble a castle, with the shortest piece of Swiss roll at the front.

3 Spread melted chocolate over the ice cream cones and then stick them to the top of the Swiss rolls with a little more chocolate. Press chocolate buttons in overlapping rows over the cones to resemble roof tiles, beginning at the widest part of the cone and working upwards, adding extra chocolate to the back of the buttons as you near the tip of the cones.

4 Reserve half of the white icing and colour the remainder light brown, then roll out on a surface dusted with icing sugar. Cut out windows, windowsills and a double door. Stick them on to the cake with a little apricot jam and mark the door with lines using a small knife. Add tiny balls of icing for door handles.

5 Knead and roll out the white icing. Cut out ghost shapes and stick them on to the windows with a little jam. Add tiny white balls for eyes and pipe black eyes and mouths with writing icing. Arrange the candles and candle-holders on the cake board.

QUICK TIPS

★ If you find that some of the chocolate buttons slide off the chocolate-covered ice cream cones, position just 2–3 rows on each cone to start with, then gradually add extra layers as the chocolate begins to set, sticking them on with more melted chocolate.

★ If you are planning to take the cake to a party venue, secure the cakes with long wooden skewers inserted through the centres of the ice cream cones, so the tops of the turrets don't topple over in transit, adding sticks at step 2.

★ Instead of novelty candles, make free-standing ghosts by shaping different size cones of white icing about 2–3.5 cm (¾–1½ inches) high. Roll out the remaining white icing and cut wavy circular shapes and drape them over the cones. Add tiny white balls for eyes and pipe on black writing icing features. Add white candles to the heads, if you like.

NOT SO SCARY
For a fairytale castle, wrap the cakes in pale pink ready-to-roll icing, add white chocolate buttons or those covered with sugar strands. Pipe on green rose stems up the brickwork and add sugar flowers. Add tiny fairy dolls or model out of coloured icing.

eyeball cakes

Makes 8
Decoration time: 25 minutes

8 bought or home-made Fairy Cakes (see page 19)
3 tablespoons smooth apricot jam
500 g (1 lb) white ready-to-roll icing
icing sugar or cornflour, for dusting
4 green glacé cherries, halved
4 yellow glacé cherries, halved
2 black liquorice twists
red paste food colouring

1 Trim the tops of the cakes to level them, if necessary. Brush the tops and sides of cakes with jam.

2 Knead the icing on a surface lightly dusted with icing sugar or cornflour, then cut it into seven pieces. Thinly roll out a piece until a little larger than a fairy cake. Drape it over a cake, smooth the top and sides and pinch each side to form an eye shape. Trim off the excess and reserve.

3 Repeat until all the cakes are covered, re-kneading all the icing trimmings to cover the final cake. Press a halved cherry into the top of each cake for the iris and add a thin slice of liquorice for the pupil.

4 Put a little red colouring on to a saucer, add a drop of water and mix together. Paint blood vessels on the top of each eyeball using a fine paintbrush. Arrange the cakes on a cake board or plate to serve.

QUICK TIPS

★ This same idea can be adapted by shaping a little white icing around halved green seedless grapes instead of the glacé cherries, adding a little liquorice for the pupil.

★ You could also serve these cakes at a doctors and nurses or pirate party.

★ If you are making your own fairy cakes, add your child's favourite flavouring (see page 19).

★ For mouths, cover cakes in red icing, in the same way, making a V-shaped indentation to one side for the top lip, then mark into two lips using the back of a small knife.

★ To make grisly-looking noses, cover triangular pieces of cake cut from a roasting tin traybake Madeira Cake (see page 20) with pale pink or green icing and shape into noses, adding nostrils by pressing the end of a wooden spoon into icing. Add small balls of leftover icing for spots and blemishes.

◄ *Decorate the party table with plastic Halloween figures or foil ghosts, pumpkins, bats and other scary shapes, all of which are available from card shops or department stores.*

pumpkin lanterns

Serves 6 children
Decoration time: 30 minutes

12 bought or home-made Fairy Cakes (see page 19)
half quantity vanilla Butter Icing (see page 23)
625 g (1¼ lb) white ready-to-roll icing
yellow and red paste food colourings
icing sugar or cornflour, for dusting
1 teaspoon smooth apricot jam

1 Trim the tops of the cakes to level them, if necessary. Sandwich the cake tops together with butter icing, then spread it thinly over the sides and bases of the cakes.

2 Colour 50 g (2 oz) of the ready-to-roll icing yellow and wrap in clingfilm. Colour the remainder orange using a little yellow and red paste food colouring. Knead well on a surface lightly dusted with icing sugar or cornflour.

3 Cut the orange icing into five pieces. Thinly roll out a piece, then place a cake pair on it so that the joins of the cake are vertical. Pleat the edges of the icing up and over the cakes and trim off any excess. Smooth the icing edges with sugar, if necessary.

4 Continue covering the cakes in the same way, re-using the trimmings to cover the final cake.

5 Thinly roll out the yellow icing and cut triangular eye shapes and jagged mouths. Stick them on to the cakes with a little apricot jam. Mix the yellow trimmings with any orange trimmings and shape into a thick rope. Mark the sides with a knife, then slice and stick on to the tops of the lanterns for pumpkin stalks. Arrange on a cake board or plate to serve.

FOR SOMETHING A LITTLE SCARIER
Fairy cakes can also be transformed into ghostie cakes by sandwiching two together and draping them with large circles of rolled-out white ready-to-roll icing so that it falls in soft folds. Pipe on black eyes and jagged mouths.

▲ *Sandwich together bought or home-made fairy cakes with butter icing and then spread it over the top and sides before wrapping in ready-to-roll icing.*

QUICK TIPS

* Chocolate or other flavoured fairy cakes can also be used (see page 19).

* If your cake board is a little battered or scratched, cover it with coloured foil or with thinly rolled out dark green ready-to-roll icing. Trim the icing flush with the edge of the cake board, then shape the trimmings into thin ropes and twist between the pumpkin lanterns, adding leaves if you like.

* As an alternative, make a single large pumpkin lantern with two pudding-basin cakes instead.

spooky spiders' webs

Makes 12
Decoration time: 30 minutes

30 x 23 x 5 cm (12 x 9 x 2 inch) home-made plain or chocolate traybake Madeira Cake (see page 20)
250 g (8 oz) smooth apricot jam
1 kg (2 lb) blue ready-to-roll icing
icing sugar or cornflour, for dusting
2 x 30 x 20 cm (12 x 8 inch) thin silver cake boards
1 tube black writing icing
1 small pack of jelly 'bursting bug' sweets
black plastic spiders

▼ *Look for tubes of black writing icing, usually sold in supermarkets in packs with three other coloured tubes. They're so easy to use that even a child could decorate these cakes.*

1 Lightly mark the cake into a 12-piece grid. Cut each piece into a web shape with scalloped edges and 6 or 7 points, using the grid as a guide for size. Don't worry about getting all the webs the same.

2 Spread the tops and sides of the cakes with jam.

3 Knead the blue ready-to-roll icing on a surface lightly dusted with icing sugar or cornflour. Tear off a piece of icing and roll it out thinly until a little larger than one of the web cakes. Drape it over the cake, smooth the top and sides with your fingertips and trim off any excess.

4 Continue covering the cakes in the same way, re-using the trimmings, until all the cakes are covered.

5 Place the cakes on the cake board. Pipe on black web details and add a bug jelly sweet to each web. Decorate the cake boards with plastic spiders, but remind the children that they're not edible.

QUICK TIPS

★ If you don't feel very confident about cutting web shapes freehand, cut a template from a piece of cardboard or a cereal packet and use this as a guide.

★ If you are very short of time, then cut the cake with a large plain round biscuit cutter and pipe on the web shape.

★ For children who don't like ready-to-roll icing, the cakes could also be coated in thick glacé icing, but spread them with jam first to keep all the crumbs in place and make simple round cakes for ease.

★ Experiment with different colours – the web background could also be green or red, even purple.

★ If you can't find bug-like sweets, then make your own out of ready-to-roll icing, adding green or red bootlace legs.

rapunzel

Serves 12 children
Decoration time: 30 minutes

double quantity pale green Butter Icing (see page 23)
28 cm (11 inch) thin round cake board
3 standard 15 cm (6 inch) bought chocolate Swiss rolls
2 bought chocolate mini Swiss rolls
750 g (1½ lb) white ready-to-roll icing
red paste food colouring
icing sugar or cornflour, for dusting
75 g (3 oz) mini marshmallows
1 tube each yellow, black and red writing icing
50 g (2 oz) yellow ready-to-roll icing
1 white chocolate button
1 pink wafer biscuit
few sugar flowers
candles and candle-holders

▲ *Spread the Swiss rolls thinly with butter icing, then wrap each one in ready-to-roll icing.*

1 Thickly spread the butter icing over the cake board. Cut 5 cm (2 inches) off one standard Swiss roll and stick the cut-off slice on to the top of the second standard Swiss roll with a little butter icing. Thinly spread butter icing over the sides and ends of all the Swiss rolls and mini rolls.

2 Knead the white ready-to-roll icing, then add a little red colouring and knead again until partially mixed, to give a marbled effect. Roll out the icing on a surface lightly dusted with icing sugar or cornflour. Cut out rectangles to cover all the Swiss rolls, measuring 20 cm (8 inches) wide and the same length as each roll. Cover the larger Swiss roll first and re-roll the trimmings as required. Cover the mini rolls last.

3 Stand the cakes close together on their ends, on the board. Place the mini rolls at the front with a gap between them for the castle entrance. Roll out the remaining pink icing trimmings and cut out a 5 cm (2 inch) square. Cut a castellated design along one edge, then stick the gate to the mini rolls with a little butter icing.

4 Decorate the tops of the castle towers with mini marshmallows stuck in place with yellow writing icing. Add a few marshmallows around the base of the castle.

5 To make Rapunzel, knead the yellow icing, then press a small ball into a round. Add the white chocolate button for the face and fold yellow icing hair around the head. Cut the remaining icing in half and shape each piece into two long ropes. Twist them together and stick them on to the side of the tallest tower with yellow writing icing. Draw Rapunzel's eyes and mouth with black and red writing icing and stick the head in position. Add tiny pieces of icing at the end of the 'plait' to suggest three strands.

6 To make the window, cut the wafer biscuit in half and cut a small piece off each end. Stick the larger window pieces in place either side of Rapunzel's head and stick one of the shorter pieces of wafer biscuit on the castle entrance to make a drawbridge. Add sugar flowers to the cake board and candles in candle-holders to the top of the turrets.

QUICK TIPS

★ If you are very short of time, leave the cake board plain and stick the Swiss rolls to it and the ready-to-roll icing to the cakes with a little smooth apricot jam. Cover the board with white chocolate buttons and sugar strands.

★ If the castles entrance droops slightly, prop it up with a piece of folded foil. Remove the foil just before serving.

cinderella

Serves 8–10 children
Decoration time: 30 minutes

2 x 15 cm (6 inch) bought or home-made, filled Victoria
   Sandwich Cakes (see page 19)
1 cinnamon bagel
4 tablespoons smooth apricot jam
20 cm (8 inch) thin round silver cake board
500 g (1 lb) white ready-to-roll icing
icing sugar or cornflour, for dusting
250 g (8 oz) pink ready-to-roll icing
1 Barbie-style doll, clothes and legs removed
1 tube white piping icing
1 sugar flower
30 g (1¼ oz) pack edible mixed coloured balls

1 Stack the cakes and top with the bagel to make the skirt. Sandwich together with a little jam, then place on the cake board. Trim a little off the top edge of the cake where it meets the bagel to smooth the line of skirt, then spread the top and sides with jam.

2 Knead and roll out the white icing on a surface lightly dusted with icing sugar or cornflour to a circle about 38 cm (15 inches) in diameter. Drape the icing over the cake so that it comes down to just over the edge of the cake board. Smooth with your fingertips dipped in icing sugar or cornflour to make a swirled skirt shape. Trim off the excess icing and reserve.

3 Knead and thinly roll out the pink icing, then trim to a 20 cm (8 inch) circle, using a plate as a guide and a fluted pastry wheel or knife. Cut the circle in half and drape each half around the top of the skirt, pleating and pressing it into place.

4 Knead the pink trimmings, roll out to a rectangle large enough to wrap around the doll. Press it on to the doll, sticking it in place with dots of jam, then trim off the excess icing and shape the front of the bodice. Press the doll into the cake and then decorate the top of the bodice with a strip of white icing cut from re-rolled trimmings with a fluted pastry wheel.

5 Pipe white icing around the join of the bodice and skirt and add a sugar flower. Pipe random dots over the white skirt and

▲ *Buy a new cheap Barbie lookalike, or raid your daughter's toybox for a doll to use. The legs can be easily twisted and removed and then pressed back into place once the cake is eaten. Alternatively, buy a specially adapted doll with a spike from a cake-decorating shop.*

stick the coloured balls in place. Add dots of icing to the front of the dress and the ears and pipe a ring around the doll's wrist. Press coloured balls on top for buttons, earrings and a bracelet.

QUICK TIPS

★ A ring doughnut could be used instead of a bagel for the top of the skirt.

★ Vary the colours and design of the doll's dress and make into Belle from *Beauty and the Beast* with a yellow and blue ballgown, or all white for Sleeping Beauty marrying her prince.

★ If you need to take the cake to a party venue, insert a couple of wooden skewers down through the sponges before icing for extra stability.

three little pigs

Serves 12 children
Decoration time: 30 minutes

**1 triple variety pack of flavoured Madeira cakes,
each 275 g (9 oz)**
30 x 25 cm (12 x 10 inch) rectangular cake board
**375 g (12 oz) bought chocolate-chip cake or other
flavoured loaf cake with sloping sides**
double quantity plain Butter Icing (see page 23)
**1 tablespoon cocoa powder dissolved in 1 tablespoon
boiling water**
green paste food colouring
50 g (2 oz) each blue, red and green ready-to-roll icing
icing sugar or cornflour, for dusting
200 g (7 oz) yellow ready-to-roll icing
150 g (5 oz) pack chocolate sticks
200 g (7 oz) luxury milk chocolate
65 g (2½ oz) chocolate fingers
125 g (4 oz) pink ready-to-roll icing
50 g (2 oz) grey ready-to-roll icing
**1 multi-pack of coloured writing icing to include black,
red, yellow and green**
50 g (2 oz) desiccated coconut

1 Put the Madeira cakes on the cake board. Cut the loaf cake into three pieces and stick one piece on top of each of the other cakes with butter icing for the roofs. Spoon one-third of the butter icing into a small bowl and flavour the remainder with the cocoa paste. Spread plain butter icing all over one of the 'houses', then colour any remaining icing green. Spread all the chocolate butter icing over the other houses.

2 Roll out the blue ready-to-roll icing on a surface lightly dusted with icing sugar or cornflour and cut a door shape for the first house. Roll out the green and red icing and add doors to the other houses with co-ordinating door knobs.

3 To make the house of straw, knead and roll out the yellow ready-to-roll icing. Cut it into 4 x 5 cm (2 inch) squares, mark lines with a knife to look like straw, then press it on to the cake.

4 To make the house of sticks, cover the house with the green door with chocolate sticks, sticking some on the roof at angles.

▲ *Make the pigs from two circles, one larger for the body and one smaller for the head. Add small balls of icing for noses and legs and triangles of icing for ears, completing with a thin rope for the tail. Make the wolf in much the same way, shaping the head into more of a snout and marking on whiskers.*

5 For the house of bricks, cut the bar of chocolate into pieces and stick them over the front and sides of the last cake, adding a double square for the chimney. Add finger biscuits for the roof.

6 Shape the pigs from three varying sized balls of pink ready-to-roll icing, large balls for the bodies, medium for the heads and small for the noses. Add tiny balls, shaped into points, for ears and larger balls for feet, each with three small cuts. Roll tiny ropes and twist into tails. Make a wolf in the same way with the grey icing, but shape the circular head into more of a snout and mark the sides of the head to look like whiskers. Position the pigs and wolf on and by the houses, sticking any parts together with water, if necessary. Mark nostrils with a knife and pipe on black eyes.

7 Spread green butter icing thinly over the cake board, colour the coconut green and scatter it over the board. Complete the houses with numbers piped on to the doors.

★ If you're short of time, leave the cake board undecorated and simply arrange the cakes on a green foil tray.

★ Three large shredded wheat breakfast cereal portions could also be used to cover the house of straw.

★ Buy pink pig sweets instead of shaping your own.

noah's ark

Serves 6 children
Decoration time: 30 minutes

2 x 275 g (9 oz) bought Madeira or layered angel cakes
5 tablespoons chocolate spread
2 bought mini chocolate-coated Swiss rolls
2 wooden skewers
18 x 10 cm (7 x 4 inch) piece cardboard or cereal packet
18 x 10 cm (7 x 4 inch) strip of foil
4 flaked chocolate bars
50 g (2 oz) dark chocolate, melted
75 g (3 oz) bag milk chocolate buttons
30 cm (12 inch) round thin cake board
1 rectangular chocolate-covered biscuit
half quantity green Butter Icing (see page 23)
single quantity blue Butter Icing (see page 23)
selection of plastic animals and trees

1 Put the cakes on a chopping board and sandwich them together along their length with 1 tablespoon of chocolate spread. Trim to the shape of a boat with a serrated knife and reserve the trimmings.

2 Cut the top and bottom off each mini Swiss roll and secure to the centre of the boat with wooden skewers, allowing the sticks to protrude above the cakes. To make the roof, make three folds in the cardboard, shape into a triangle and secure with sticky tape. Wrap tightly with foil and tape in place. Make two small holes on the underside and then press the roof over the wooden skewers.

3 Spread the top and sides of the boat with the remaining chocolate spread. Cut the flaked chocolate bars into quarters lengthways – don't worry if they break. Press pieces of the chocolate on to the boat until the sides are completely covered.

4 Lift the roof off the ark, spread it with melted chocolate and press on the chocolate buttons for roof tiles, beginning at the base and working upwards. When the first side is complete, put it button-side down on a plate and cover the second side. Chill the roof for 10 minutes.

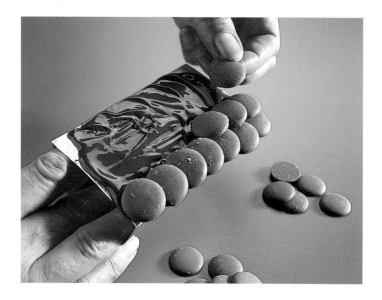

▲ *Make a roof shape from cardboard cut from a cereal packet, cover with foil, then spread with melted chocolate and decorate with chocolate button 'roof tiles'.*

5 Position the ark on the cake board and use the reserved cake trimmings to make a small island, positioning it close enough to the ark for a chocolate-covered biscuit gangplank to rest against the boat and land. Cover the cake island and some of the board with green butter icing. Swirl blue butter icing around the boat for the sea.

6 Arrange the plastic animals on the ark, pressing the legs of the larger ones into the cake. Position some animals and plastic trees on the island and a couple on the gangplank. Place the ark roof in position.

QUICK TIPS

★ The ark can also be spread with chocolate Butter Icing (see page 23) instead of chocolate spread, if preferred.

★ Use any very broken pieces of flaked chocolate bar around the back of the ark.

★ Sea and land could also be made by spreading jam over the cake board and island and adding desiccated coconut coloured with a little blue and green food colouring.

santa's sack

Serves 10 children
Decoration time: 25 minutes

18 x 10 cm (7 x 4 inch) bought rich fruit cake
25 x 20 cm (10 x 8 inch) thin silver cake board
2 tablespoons smooth apricot jam
750 g (1½ lb) red ready-to-roll icing
icing sugar or cornflour, for dusting
75 g (3 oz) white ready-to-roll icing
selection of boiled sweets
few foil-covered chocolate coins

1 Put the cake on the cake board and spread the sides with apricot jam, reserving a little.

2 Knead the red icing, then roll out thinly on a surface lightly dusted with icing sugar or cornflour. Cut 2 rectangles 19 x 16 cm (7½ x 6½ inches) and press them on to the long sides of the cake. Re-roll the trimmings and cut 2 x 13 cm (5½ inch) squares. Press them on to the short ends of the cake.

3 Smooth the icing over the cake with your fingertips dusted in cornflour and press the icing joins together. Don't worry if the icing sags down the sides a little; it will make the sack look more interesting. Smooth the top edge of the icing to give a wavy effect, then fill the top of the sack with sweets and coins. Roll out the white icing and stamp out tiny stars. Stick them on to the long sides of the sack with a little jam.

► *Decorate the outside of the sack with icing cut into tiny stars or holly leaves with metal cutters. Tiny cutters can be bought from specialist cake-decorating shops or cookshops, where they may be labelled 'aspic cutters'. Choose mixed sets of shapes in lidded containers, if you can, as these are less likely to get lost.*

QUICK TIPS

★ If you would like to make your own cake, use a 15 cm (6 inch) rich fruit cake, Madeira or chocolate cake.

★ If you are not a fan of fruit cake, use 2 x 275 g (9 oz) bought Madeira cakes and sandwich the long edges together with jam or butter icing.

★ If you are entertaining a big crowd for Christmas, simply increase the size of cake and the number of decorations.

★ For marzipan lovers, cover the cake with rolled-out marzipan, trimmed to the same size as the sides of the cake, and then ice as in the recipe. Alternatively, colour marzipan and use this on its own, just like ready-to-roll icing.

father christmas faces

Serves 12 children
Decoration time: 20 minutes

12 bought or home-made Fairy Cakes (see page 19)
single quantity plain Butter Icing (see page 23)
100 g (3½ oz) luxury white chocolate, coarsely grated
24 dried cranberries
24 sugar-coated chocolate chips or mini candy-covered
**   chocolate drops**
125 g (4 oz) red ready-to-roll icing
icing sugar or cornflour, for dusting
1 tube red writing icing

1 Trim the tops off the cakes to level them, if necessary, then spread them with butter icing. Holding each cake over a plate, sprinkle with the grated white chocolate. Place on a serving plate or cake board.

2 Press on cranberry cheeks and chocolate-drop eyes.

3 Knead the red ready-to-roll icing and roll out thinly on a surface lightly dusted with icing sugar or cornflour. Cut triangles about 5 cm (2 inches) long and press them on to the tops of the cakes, sticking them with a little more butter icing and curling the tops slightly.

4 Pipe on red mouths with writing icing.

QUICK TIP

★ To turn an everyday tea into a special occasion, keep a handy supply of home-made fairy cakes in the freezer and decorate while still frozen.

▲ *Look out for festive paper or colourful foil cup-cake cases in large supermarkets, specialist cake-decorating shops or cookshops from late November.*

penguins' igloo

Serves 8 children
Decoration time: 30 minutes

3 tablespoons smooth apricot jam
2 x 15 cm (6 inch) bought or home-made filled
  Victoria sandwich cakes(see page 19)
28 cm (11 inch) thin round cake board, plain or iced
500 g (1 lb) white ready-to-roll icing
icing sugar or cornflour, for dusting
1 bought mini Swiss roll
4 tablespoons desiccated coconut
250 g (8 oz) black ready-to-roll icing
25 g (1 oz) red ready-to-roll icing
14 edible silver balls

1 Spread a little jam over the top of one of the cakes and place the second cake on top. Using a small serrated knife, cut away the edges of the top cake to make a domed igloo shape. Spread the top and sides of the cakes with jam and place just off centre on the cake board.

▼ *To shape a penguin, simply make two balls of black icing, one slightly larger than the other, for the head and body. Add a flattened rope shape for the wings, a round white oval for the tummy, edible silver balls for the eyes and a tiny triangle of red icing for the beak.*

2 Knead the white ready-to-roll icing and roll out on a surface lightly dusted with icing sugar or cornflour to a 25 cm (10 inch) circle. Drape the icing over the cakes and smooth it over the top and sides. Trim off the excess and knead the trimmings.

3 Cut the mini roll in half and put one piece on top of the other, sticking it in place with jam. Roll out a little of the remaining white ready-to-roll icing, and use to cover the mini roll, pressing a doorway shape in one end. Butt the mini roll up against the igloo, sticking it in place with jam. With a small knife, mark on snow bricks all over the igloo and tunnel entrance.

4 Shape the remaining white icing into small balls and set aside. Sprinkle coconut around the base of the igloo.

5 To make the penguins, shape black ready-to-roll icing into 6–7 small balls and the same number of slightly larger balls. Press the small balls on top of the larger ones to make the penguins' heads and bodies. Roll the remaining black icing into 7 ropes, each about 5 cm (2 inches) long. Flatten the ropes with your fingertips, shaping the ends into points, and wrap them around the penguin bodies for wings. Add tiny triangles of red icing for beaks and silver balls for eyes.

6 Press 6–7 of the smaller white balls of icing into ovals and then press on to the penguins' tummies. Arrange the penguins on the cake with small balls of white icing for snowballs.

QUICK TIPS

✱ If you would like to make your own cakes, see page 19. You will need to make two pairs of cakes, and fill them with butter icing or jam.

✱ To cover the cake board, use 250 g (8 oz) blue ready-to-roll icing and stick it on to the cake board with a little smooth apricot jam, spread around the outer edges of the board.

✱ Don't forget to wash your hands before adding the white balls of icing to the penguin tummies or they will turn a rather grubby grey.

christmas trees

Serves 12 children
Decoration time: 25 minutes

30 x 23 x 5 cm (12 x 9 x 2 inch) home-made traybake
    Madeira Cake (see page 20)
quadruple quantity green Butter Icing (see page 23)
12 blue foil-covered chocolates
1 tube red writing icing
1 tube yellow writing icing
2 tubes or packets of candy-covered chocolate drops

1 Cut the cake into three strips measuring 23 x 10 cm
(9 x 4 inches), then cut each strip into three triangles, each
10 cm (4 inches) high. Top and tail the triangles so that there is
only a half triangle of sponge left at the top and bottom of each
strip, then butt halves together with a little butter icing.

2 Spread the tops and sides of the cakes thinly with butter icing
to stick the crumbs in place, then spread with a thicker layer of
icing. Arrange the triangles on a cake board or plate, then place
chocolate sweets at the base of each one for the tubs.

3 Pipe on tree garlands with red and yellow writing icing and
press on sweets for decorations.

QUICK TIPS

★ If you don't want to buy sweets specially for the tubs, cut
the sponge trimmings into squares and spread with a little
remaining of the butter icing to stick them into place, or wrap
in red ready-to-roll icing.

★ Butter-iced trees can be frozen in advance, but it's best to add
the writing icing and sweets once they have thawed.

▲ *Top and tail the sponge triangle shapes to minimize the
amount of wastage.*

twelfth night crown

Serves 8 children
Decoration time: 20 minutes

18 cm (7 inch) bought or home-made Victoria Sandwich
    Cake (see page 19)
single quantity orange Butter Icing (see page 23)
23 cm (9 inch) thin round cake board
4 tablespoons sugar strands
500 g (1 lb) yellow ready-to-roll icing
icing sugar or cornflour, for dusting
16 black jelly beans
9 clear fruit sweets
1 tube yellow writing icing

1 Sandwich the cakes together with some of the butter icing.
Place them on the cake board and spread butter icing thinly over
the sides of the cake and thickly over the top. Sprinkle sugar
strands over the top.

2 Knead and roll out the yellow ready-to-roll icing on a surface
lightly dusted with icing sugar or cornflour. Trim to a 60 x 8 cm
(24 x 3½ inch) rectangle. Scallop the top using a plain 6 cm
(2½ inch) biscuit cutter, then carefully press the strip of icing
around the edge of the cake.

3 Knead the trimmings and shape into a 60 cm (24 inch) long
rope. Press the rope on to the base of the cake, trimming the
ends, if necessary, and sticking it in place with a little butter
icing. Spread the remaining butter icing over the icing rope to
resemble a fur trim. Decorate with black jelly beans.

4 Stick the clear fruit sweets on to the crown for jewels using a
generous quantity of writing icing.

> **TWELFTH NIGHT CELEBRATIONS**
> For a child born just after Christmas, it can be fun to
> celebrate Twelfth night. Traditionally, a dried pea or bean
> was added to the cake before baking and whoever finds it
> in their slice is king or queen for the day.

▲ *Transform a strip of yellow ready-to-roll icing into a
scalloped-edged crown by using a small round plain plastic
or metal biscuit cutter.*

QUICK TIPS

★ The top of the cake could also be covered with rumpled red or
blue ready-to-roll icing to give the impression of velvet.

★ Don't add the clear fruit sweets until the last moment, as they
can dissolve if left to stand for any length of time. You need to
be quite generous with the writing icing or you will find that
the sweets slide off the crown.

christmas reindeer

Serves 12 children
Decoration time: 25 minutes

**30 x 23 x 5 cm (12 x 9 x 2 inch) home-made chocolate
traybake Madeira Cake (see page 20)**
40 x 30 cm (16 x 12 inch) thin rectangular cake board
double quantity chocolate Butter Icing (see page 23)
125 g (4 oz) light brown ready-to-roll icing
icing sugar or cornflour, for dusting
40 g (1½ oz) red ready-to-roll icing
15 g (½ oz) white ready-to-roll icing
few chocolate sticks
sifted icing sugar, to serve

1 Put the cake on a chopping board and cut it in half to make two 23 x 15 cm (9 x 6 inch) rectangles. Cut one of these halves in half again to make 2 x 15 x 11 cm (6 x 4½ inch) rectangles. Finally, cut one of the smaller pieces into 3 strips, each 11 x 5 cm (4½ x 2 inches).

2 Arrange the larger piece of cake on the cake board for the reindeer body, cutting off the corners to make a curved shape. Use the next largest cake for the head and cut off the corners to make a curved shape. Overlap the head and body and tuck the cake trimmings under the top of the head to support it.

3 Use 2 of the smaller cakes to make the legs, cutting the tops at a slight angle so that legs are not completely upright. Use the remaining piece of cake to lengthen the reindeer head.

4 Stick the cut edges of the cake together with butter icing, where necessary, then use the rest to cover the top and sides of the cake. Wipe any excess icing off the board with kitchen paper.

5 Knead the light brown ready-to-roll icing and roll out a little on a surface lightly dusted with icing sugar or cornflour. Use to cover the ends of the legs to make hooves. Trim off the excess. Roll out the remaining light brown icing and cut oval ears about 7 cm (3 inches) long and a smiling mouth. Place them on the cake, pinching the ends of the ears together.

6 Shape the red icing into a ball and place it on the head for the nose. Shape the white icing into two ovals, and press them on to

▲ *There's no need for a fancy animal-shaped tin to bake this cake – you just need an everyday roasting tin and a knife to cut and shape the cake when cooked.*

the head for eyes, sticking on small pieces of chocolate stick for eyeballs. Add whole and halved pieces of chocolate for antlers. Shield the cake with a piece of paper and dust the cake board with sifted icing sugar just before serving.

QUICK TIPS

* As there are so many cut edges of sponge, you may find it easier to spread a thin layer of butter icing all over the cake to stick the crumbs in place, then to spread a thicker layer over the top.

* If you don't want to open a large pack of white ready-to-roll icing just to the make the eyes, then use 2 white chocolate buttons instead.

* As the amounts of ready-to-roll icing are so small, you may prefer to divide and colour a pack of white instead.

index

acknowledgements

Photographer: Dave Jordan
Home Economist: Sara Lewis
Executive Editor: Nicola Hill
Editor: Abi Rowsell

Executive Art Editor: Leigh Jones
Designer: Jo Tapper
Picture Researcher: Jennifer Veall
Production Controller: Lucy Woodhead